# How to avoid the
# 77 biggest
# mistakes made by
# property investors

*by*

*Rhett Lewis*

**Grosvenor House
Publishing Limited**

This book is published by
Grosvenor House Publishing Ltd
28-30 High Street, Guildford, Surrey, GU1 3HY.
www.grosvenorhousepublishing.co.uk

A CIP record for this book
is available from the British Library

ISBN 978-1-906645-60-1

# Welcome to a New Approach to Investing

In less than a decade the Buy-to-Let opportunity in the UK has become a significant industry, evidenced by the flurry of TV programmes showing hundreds of ordinary people creating extraordinary wealth.

Rhett Lewis Property Investments has also enjoyed extraordinary success, building an enviable reputation and a sound platform for future growth. Our team has worked tirelessly to get us to where the company is today, in a relatively short space of time, and my vision – looking at the opportunities today, systemising our formula and strategically planning our future – is ensuring that we continue to thrive and develop from our solid financial base. My purpose is single minded: to share our formula for success by involving as many people as we can in property investing.

We offer rewarding services for investors at entry level, ranging from straightforward, passive investments all the way up to large-scale portfolios. I invite you to join us on our mission to create more wealth for all, and I hope you enjoy reading the comprehensive information that I have prepared for you within this book.

Regards

Rhett Lewis
Managing Director

# Contents

# CONTENTS

# CONTENTS

# CONTENTS

# CONTENTS

# MISTAKE 1

# Falling in love with the property

When purchasing an investment property many people forget that they are not going to live in it themselves. They buy the property with their own expectations in mind. They care what the curtains look like and if the kitchen has stainless steel appliances and whether the colour scheme is to their taste. But an investment property is just that – an investment property: a means to wealth creation.

I have to confess, I fell in love with our first investment property. Notwithstanding the fact that I had just completed a course and understood the concept of falling in love with the numbers first, I couldn't help but be excited about buying my first property. I had spent my working life living from pay cheque to pay cheque, scratching to pay each bill on time and never managing to get ahead. Sound familiar? When I purchased my first investment property, I was so excited about owning my very own property I fell head over heels in love with it.

At the time, I failed to understand that the tenant used the house, not me. In fact our current tenant in that property has now been there for several years. He is a typical single male, a smoker and untidy with it. I am sure he doesn't appreciate the quality and expense of the house. I used to cringe every time I thought about it but he pays the rent every month so I can't complain.

Focus on the area in which you are purchasing your investment property and ask local lettings managers about the features tenants look for in a rental property. A lettings manager can give you a wealth of information about what tenants want, so listen closely. If you are purchasing a property in a hot climate, make sure your investment property has air conditioning. If your investment property is targeted at families, then prospective tenants will appreciate a dishwasher and a well-fenced backyard for the children to play in. If your investment property is an apartment, then consider balconies and internal laundries. Target properties that tenants like to live in and ensure they have the features they are looking for. For example, you might dream of having a property with 12 foot ceilings but a tenant probably won't care.

A dishwasher would be more sought after than high ceilings and that dishwasher would earn you more rent, therefore giving you a better return on your investment.

So it is really easy to avoid this mistake. Purchase properties in which tenants will want to live and try not to care about the furnishings in the house. Quite often your first property, aside from being quite emotional, can highlight the features you do not have in your own home, as it did for me.

Here's my tip: stay focused on the bigger picture. You are buying this investment property to create financial wealth for yourself. By finding out what it is that tenants want, you will avoid the emotional roller coaster ride. It does get easier with each additional property purchase you make thereafter. Practice makes perfect.

# MISTAKE 2

# Not seeking expert advice

It's amazing how many investors purchase property without consulting their accountants or finance brokers until the deal is done. To have a panel of experts to refer to can be the difference between buying a great investment or a lemon. How can you predict the impact of your investment purchase on your finances if you do not consult with experts? What effect will the property purchase have on your taxable income? How much money can you actually borrow? How much of your income will that new investment property require each week?

Although this is not a mistake I have made personally, I have seen other investors make it countless times. My mentors have helped me not to make this mistake. They have even provided me with a great advantage: to use the same experts they use. I have found that better experts increased my level of knowledge and allowed me to leverage my opportunities to a greater extent.

People regularly fail to seek advice from mortgage brokers or bank managers. I have witnessed this on many occasions: someone purchases an investment property at auction, hands over a sizeable deposit only then to discover they cannot obtain the finance to complete the transaction. If you have made this mistake yourself, or know of someone who has, you would know that a conversation with a mortgage broker or bank manager before you sign the contract and part with your deposit would have saved you many sleepless nights.

I can't stress enough the importance of having experts as part of your team. One of the most fundamental questions to ask your panel of experts is whether they are investors themselves. How can they possibly know all the minutiae of property investing if they do not practise it themselves?

Look at property investing as a business and the experts as your employees. You don' t need to involve yourself with payroll taxes and staff amenities and you only need to pay them when you use them. If you are very worried about their fees then you should not be a property investor - if the advice saves you thousands of pounds then you shouldn't be concerned about parting with a few hundred pounds.

If the expert is not working for you, them stop using them or her and find someone who will work with you and give you great advice. Do you think Donald Trump made his billions by knowing everything himself? Absolutely not! He relies on the expert knowledge of solicitors, accountants and financiers to grow his wealth. You too can do the same.

Before you purchase an investment property, speak with your accountant and ask him/her what the impact of the purchase will be. Ask whether buying it in your name or a trust or company is better for you. Let them know your long-term intentions for the property so they can advise you accordingly. They must be able to guide you from their own experience within the boundaries of the law.

Here's my tip: seek expert advice before – not after - you purchase your investment property.

# MISTAKE 3

# Not having an exit strategy

An exit strategy is the back-up plan for when things go horribly wrong and you need to find a way out without suffering huge financial and emotional loss. So many investors don't even know what an exit strategy is, let alone what to do if things go wrong.

Here are just some of the things investors do not consider:
What happens if you can't find a tenant?
What happens if the property burns down?
What happens if you lose your job and can't pay the mortgage?
What if interest rates go up?
What if your personal circumstances change?
What happens if your tenant doesn't pay the rent?

If you haven't devised an exit strategy for these types of situations, then you're not properly managing your investment. If you don't know how you are going to handle each and every disaster that could potentially come along then you'll go round the twist worrying about the possibilities. Having an exit strategy will give you peace of mind and allow you to sleep at night. When investing in property you are dealing with big money and it's not worth jeopardising your financial situation, lifestyle or relationships by incessantly worrying about situations that you have not planned for.

Many people contact me wanting to participate in our property mentoring programs yet their spouses or partners are afraid to borrow money. In fact they can't stand the thought of getting into more debt than they already have. The reason for this is that they haven't been educated into understanding the difference between good debt and bad debt. Once properly understood, people's fear of good debt quickly disappears and they begin to welcome good debt with open arms. Until this fear is overcome it just isn't possible to build a successful portfolio. Nine times out of ten it is people's lack of understanding, education and exit planning that creates fear or causes their ideas to fail. Once people have been educated and understand all the dynamics that lead to successful property investing, they gain the confidence to be able to appreciate just how low risk property investing can be.

I have known people who have jumped into the property market because their friends have done so, or to 'keep up with the Jones's. They buy something without fully understanding the consequences. The exit strategy is what gives you peace of mind today and tomorrow. Here are some suggestions for your exit strategy.

**Insurance** –this includes building, contents and landlord's insurance: if your investment property is worth hundreds of thousands of pounds and has an uncertain tenant, you would be wise to invest the few hundred pounds per year on insurances to cover the risk(s).

As part of your mortgage your financier will require you to have building insurance. However building insurance does not cover you for any of the contents such as carpets, window furnishings, light fittings etc. Therefore you will need to obtain contents insurance as well. Your insurance company or broker will advise you as to the level of contents cover you will require. Some landlord insurance policies include a minimal amount for landlord's contents, and it is worth checking with your broker whether this is included.

Most comprehensive landlords insurance policies will cover a number of 'what-ifs', including: the cost of any damage to the property caused by the tenant; the property being destroyed; the tenant squatting and not paying their rent; the tenant leaving without paying rent; loss of rent while any damage is repaired and legal liability. Should the tenant or the tenant's visitors misbehave or be injured in any way, at least you know your insurance policy will cover it. You will need to consult with an expert insurance agent to make sure you have the correct insurance coverage for your property.

If you purchase an investment property as part of a complex, building insurance is generally covered under the management company's insurance policy. But make sure the policy is adequate for your peace of mind and includes areas such as your car park and/or storage areas on your part of the title.

Here's my tip: you will need to read the terms and conditions of your policy in detail as insurance companies vary greatly in what they will cover. And remember, if you pay peanuts, you are bound to get monkeys so make sure your policy has all the necessary inclusions.

**Fixing interest rates** – a method for guarding against interest rate rises is to fix your interest rates for three, five or ten years. The fixed interest rate is generally slightly higher than the variable rate but if interest rate peace of mind is what you want then this might be for you. If you are nervous about interest rate fluctuations, then fix all or part of your loan to ensure consistency in your costs. In this way you will know that the major portion of your property's expenses will be fixed for that period of time. Be careful however not to fix interest rates just before they are about to come down.

About three years ago fixed interest rates were at an all time low at 5.99%, which was lower than the 6.3% variable rate. I was able to fix my mortgages at 5.99% for five years, which was beneficial when rates increased to 7.3%. With falling rates, I do forgo the benefits, but I know exactly where I stand with regard to my monthly payments, and I have been comfortable with the rate at which I fixed.

**Lack of cash flow** – people's circumstances change all the time and a way to minimise any change from affecting your cash flow, and hence your ability to pay out-of-pocket mortgage payments and expenses, is to plan ahead.

I keep a bucket of money in an account for such occasions. If, for some reason, I can't afford the mortgage for that month due to it being untenanted (it has never happened but just in case) that money is used, which gives me peace of mind knowing that if anything goes wrong, I will not run the risk of losing the investment property.

Here's my tip: write down every fear you may have about investing in property and try to come up with an exit strategy for each situation that could arise. You may need to seek expert advice to check the feasibility of some of your strategies. If you cannot overcome a fear by developing a workable exit strategy, even with the advice of experts, it may be best not to proceed with the purchase. You need to feel comfortable at all times with every aspect of the purchase.

# 4
## MISTAKE 4

# Not crunching the numbers properly

Most property investors who fail, do so because they only 'guestimate' the cost of things without fully understanding the implications of their financial position.

When considered properly the numbers give an investor a financial understanding of the true cost of an investment; whether it is in negative cash-flow, neutral or positive and what the impact will be on their lifestyle. For example, an investor I know purchased a negatively geared property in a major city, thinking it would have a shortfall of £100 per week. On proper analysis of the numbers the investor discovered the property was costing closer to £260 per week (out of pocket). This investor was also wondering why the bank would not lend him more money for further property purchases.

When I started out I didn't fully understand the 'power of the numbers' and what that actually meant to me on a weekly basis. It wasn't until I purchased some analysis software that I could fully appreciate how much a property would cost me each week and gain a clear understanding of the numbers. Using the software allowed me to understand how getting into property investing would impact on my lifestyle. It made the numbers 'real' for me.

From then on, before putting in any offers, I would crunch the numbers on each and every property deal. The two variables I played with the most were the purchase price and the rent. If the asking price and the market rent of the property did not meet my requirements I would offer less or increase the rent to see if it changed the bottom line. If the numbers still didn't meet my requirements, even after tweaking, I would walk away and look for something else. Having completed due diligence I would know what was fair market rent and value for a property.

The software allowed me to play with different scenarios so I could see what I needed to achieve in the purchase price and rent for the deal to stack up. There are a number of software packages on the market that allow you to 'crunch the numbers' on existing and potential property deals. For a small amount of money, software could potentially save you from making a huge financial mistake. Before buying any investment property, I always run the numbers through the software to work out what it will cost me each week.

Some analysis software allows you to add several properties at once in order to obtain an overview of the whole portfolio. For example, I looked at a block of units with an excellent rental return. The block of units was on the market for £500,000 and the rental return was approximately £70,000 per year. There was room to increase the rent. I started to enter the figures into my software. However when I entered in all the costs, including the very high council rates, it made the deal negative. At the time I was looking for cash flow opportunities and, had I not crunched the numbers, I would have purchased a block of units that would actually have cost me around £120 per week.

Here's my tip: crunching the numbers could save you thousands of pounds so if you are going to get into property investing, purchase some quality software as it will be the cheapest asset you buy. Not understanding the rate of return on a property purchase is like gambling, and in there are too many zeros to risk getting it wrong.

# MISTAKE 5

# Not doing your homework

Due diligence is the research carried out prior to making the purchase. It helps the investor decide whether the property is a good buy or a 'goodbye'. Many investors talk to the selling agent, ask a few questions and then make their decision. If they can obtain finance for the property, the transaction goes ahead. There are so many horror stories from investors who did not do their due diligence on the property before they bought it.

Here are some questions investors do not consider:

Where and how far away are the schools, shopping centres, medical practitioners, facilities and transport?
What are the local council's future plans for the area?
What kinds of developments are being planned for the area?
Who lives in the street?
What has been the capital growth of the area over the past twelve months, five and ten years?
What is the predicted growth for the future?
Has the property been tenanted before? If so, for how long?
Is it the type of property that is sought after by tenants?
What is the vacancy rate of the area?

For example, one investor I came across purchased a property without knowing what the neighbours were planning. Three months after his purchase, the neighbours sold up to a developer who started building a five-storey apartment block next door. Had the investor done some due diligence prior to purchasing the property, there would have been no surprises and he could have chosen whether to proceed with the transaction or not.

Another first-time investor purchased an investment property, a block of four units, on the advice of someone else only to find out later that the council rates were £1,000 more than expected, and that the whole block needed a renovation that ended up costing £50,000 more than was originally quoted. In addition to this, two of the apartments were tenanted by drunks and local letting managers refused to manage the property.

A new investor used a buyer's advocate to purchase an investment property because he was time poor. He paid nearly £8,000 to the advocate for finding him the deal, which was an old block of units in the countryside, a considerable distance away, that was 30 years old and had never been renovated. The investor came seeking my opinion after the deal was done. My first question was whether he had seen the property and whether he knew what condition it was in. Other than a few photographs he could not give me any information, as he had not seen it. I suggested it would be useful for him (being a new property investor) to go and have a look at it. The response I received was very negative. He questioned why he should spend money on an airline ticket to see the property.

He had spent hundreds of thousands of pounds purchasing an investment property as well as a fee to someone for finding him the property, a property that turned out to be something less than it was cracked up to be, and all because he couldn't find the time to undertake his own due diligence.

A good start would be to drive around the area in question to see what it is like. Try and imagine that you are a potential tenant and ask yourself whether the area has nearby transport links, schools and shops. There are many websites where you can obtain free data about the demographics of the area that you are investigating. These websites will give you all sorts of valuable information, from the population to how many people rent in that area. As these websites are free there are no excuses for not consulting them.

Here are my tips:

**One:** Conduct your own due diligence on each and every property before you buy it. It will help you validate the information you will get from sales agents and other people who have a vested interest in the sale. Once you know how, undertaking due diligence is not as difficult as you might think. In fact it's quite easy. Just remember shortcuts will cost you in the end, so do it properly and thoroughly.

**Two:** When choosing the right area to invest in, look for an area where the rental population is greater than 30% as it will help ensure there are enough prospective tenants to go around.

**Three:** To find out about the planned infrastructure of the area check the local council's website, which is usually full of great information. Don't be afraid to ring the council and speak to the town planner or business development manager. They will inform you of the future plans the council has for the area, and you will be amazed at how helpful they are to investors. Finally, don't forget to ask if your neighbours are planning to sell to a developer who wants to build a five-storey building next door!

**Four:** A number of websites offer information on capital growth in particular areas of interest, but you will need to be careful that the owner of the website is getting information from a reputable source. The type of information you will be able to obtain from these sites will give you a guide as to the sort of capital growth that has occurred over the past 12 months plus an indication as to how it will track in the future. Magazines also provide valuable information on growth rates etc. and there are many good property analysis companies which, for a small fee, will provide capital growth projection reports. Capital growth is important because it is the factor that creates serious wealth for property investors.

**Five:** How do you know if your property has been tenanted before? ASK!

The sales agent should have a history of the property or at least know who the lettings manager is. Contact that lettings manager and ask about the property.

Find out whether they liked managing the property (this will give you an idea of how much work there is for the property manager). As a rule, lettings managers do not like properties that require constant maintenance as it takes up a lot of their time.

You can also ask the property manager about the vacancy rate in the area, which will give you an idea as to how long the property will take to rent out. As an investor, you do not want to have your property untenanted for months and then have to lower your rent to get someone into the property quickly. A tenant paying for the mortgage is better than you having to pay for it, so don't be afraid to lower the rent to get a tenant in. Ask the property manager what it is that tenants in the area are looking for, as this will help with sourcing a property that will rent very well. Also remember that booms don't last forever, so if there is a rental glut you want your property to be the most sought after in any market. Having the features that tenants are seeking will help ensure your property remains constantly tenanted.

# Not having a proper rent collection system in place

You've done all your homework. You've bought a property in a good location at a great price. You've found your very first tenants. Most people would think that the next step is to kick back and start enjoying the returns on their investment. Unfortunately 'most people' are in for a rude shock. This shock usually comes in the form of logging-in to your Internet banking service and seeing that the latest rent instalment has not been paid. At this stage the penny probably starts to drop and it tells you one thing: "This is going to be very hard work!"

People respond to their first introduction to the joys of 'tenancy turmoil' in two ways. Many think: "If this is what is all about then I want no further part in it!" Others decide to throw themselves heart and soul into managing and maintaining their properties, while also running a debt collection service on the side! This is all well and good until they realise one day that their anticipated relaxed lifestyle of a property investor has turned into a 12 hour a day merry go round of dealing with tenants, tradesmen, banks and whoever else demands a slice of the action!

The most stressful part of property management, and therefore the one that landlords dread most, is making sure that the rent gets paid every month. Most people do not like chasing other people for money and many landlords have given up on their dreams for precisely this reason. This is a great pity, since it doesn't have to be this way at all. My advice to all prospective landlords is to make sure that they familiarise themselves with the basic principles of tenancy management as it relates to rent collection before starting out. Some of the basic techniques that can be adopted to streamline the rent collection process:

- Do your homework long before the first rent check is due. Renting to tenants with good references and solid credit histories can save you a lot of hassle later on. You should therefore make sure that you run credit checks and chase up all references provided.
- Familiarise yourself with the relevant laws governing property rentals in your area and ensure that your rental contracts offer you the maximum possible legal recourse against late payment and defaulting. Explain the legal options open to you to new tenants at the beginning of each tenancy. Possible legal action tends to focus minds!
- Do not, if at all possible, receive payment by cash or personal cheque. Being paid by Standing Order is not foolproof but it does make it slightly more difficult for the tenant not to pay.
- It is possible to outsource the process of rent collection to a rent collection agency. There are, almost certainly, a few operating in your area. Check with other landlords to find out which one they would recommend.

**Remember:** your properties should work for you, not the other way around! One of the best ways to ensure this is to design a low maintenance rent collection system to ensure that you get your money on time, every time.

## MISTAKE 7

# Not considering all
# the mortgage options

There are few things as confusing to prospective landlords as the different mortgage options and deals to choose from. There is, however, one option that some prospective landlords discount without having considered its merits: The interest only mortgage.

When you take out an interest only mortgage you pay only the monthly interest due on the loan while the capital amount still remains due at the end of the mortgage term. This means that your mortgage payments are not repayments as such, but rather a kind of rental payment for the credit that has been extended to you.

Interest only mortgages have historically been very popular in times of high house price growth since they allowed people to 'get on the housing ladder' at a relatively low monthly rate. Customers worked on the assumption that the growth in property value would, over time, yield enough cash to repay the bank and still make them a tidy profit. But in the current house price climate most people would consider taking out an interest only mortgage as a rather risky venture.

There are still, however, some very good reasons why prospective landlords should seriously consider interest only mortgages as a legitimate option for financing their investments. The main advantages are:

**Lower monthly payments:** Since only the interest on the capital is paid, the monthly amount payable by a landlord can be significantly lower than with a traditional mortgage. This fact can help a landlord to enter a particularly profitable location with high rental yields, which is something that may not have been possible with the larger monthly commitment of a repayment mortgage. Obviously, the landlord should be certain that the rental yields will cover the interest and allow something to be set aside for the eventual repayment of the capital cost.

**To free up funds for diversification and investment:** The fact that a portion of your monthly rental income will not have to go towards servicing capital repayment means that it can work for you! Having this money available can help you climb the property ladder more quickly as you can invest it in ways that will maximise investment returns or that will extend your portfolio more swiftly than would otherwise have been possible. This must obviously be approached with considerable caution since you have to remember that the capital will eventually have to be repaid. However if you are a confident and skilled investor, this option can give you some funds to work with. Many 'buy to let' empires have been built by the judicious use of such funds!

**Lower tax bills:** If you are a landlord you can offset the interest you pay on your mortgage against your income tax bill. In other words, the higher the proportion of interest repayments in your monthly mortgage bill, the more you can save on tax. Using this equation, interest only mortgages obviously carry the greatest tax advantages.

Weighing mortgage options is never easy and your eventual decision will to a great extent depend on what is right for you in your particular circumstances. Make sure, however, that you take a good look at all the options. This means that you should, amongst other things, investigate whether an interest only mortgage might be entirely suited to your specific circumstances.

## MISTAKE 8

# Failing to do proper tax planning

We all know the old saying about death and taxes being the only two certainties in life. There is no reason however that tax should be the death of your business. One of the most common mistakes that new investors make is to neglect to do proper tax planning from the outset. It is no exaggeration to say that this mistake has led to the untimely demise of many a budding property empire. So how can you minimise your exposure to HM Revenue (and Customs) while at the same time keeping everything legal and above board? Here are a few suggestions:

- **Get expert tax advice.** Tax Law is a very complex and constantly changing area. Most of us know when bigger changes to the tax system occur but it takes a special kind of person to wade through, and make sense of, all the reams of tax related papers issued by the various government ministries and agencies. These 'special people' are called tax experts and you must consult one before you begin your career as an investor.

- **Make sure that you claim tax relief as appropriate.** Your buy to let business is exactly that: a business. This means that legitimate business expenses can be offset against your tax bill. Your tax advisor will help you with determining which expenses you can offset against your profit but tax relief can probably, at the very least, be claimed for the following: mortgage interest, repairs, insurance, letting agency fees and advisory fees (see above!).

- **Plan ahead.** There are some types of taxes that may not concern you at the moment but that could eat into your net worth in the future. Chief among these is Capital Gains Tax, a mechanism used by HM Revenue to claim a share of the profit on the sale of a property as tax. You should therefore carefully plan your exit strategy for when or if the day comes to sell your properties. There are various ways to minimise the potential impact of Capital Gains Tax but these can only be effective if they are planned beforehand.

One of the very best ways to ensure that you do not pay too much tax is to ensure that your business is structured in the right way. It may be that you will be better off establishing a Limited Company or a partnership. There are some very real tax advantages to doing this. Setting up a tailor-made business structure may seem like hard work but the long-term benefits can be great. Make sure that you speak to your tax advisor and other experts about ways to structure your business for optimal tax efficiency and growth. Conversely, one of the easiest ways to pay enormous amounts of tax is to do nothing and to conduct business in the same way as you have always done. Avoid this trap by doing everything in your power to ensure that you pay unto Caesar what is his, but not a penny more!

# MISTAKE 9

# Failing to do proper market research

It is amazing how people sometimes rush blindly into making some of the biggest purchases of their lives. The area of is, sadly, no stranger to this phenomenon. Many property investors use very flimsy criteria when deciding in which area to invest. This often leads to some potentially disastrous investment decisions, such as:

- Buying in your local area without giving any thought to critical factors like tenant demand and rental returns.
- Buying in an area purely because you have some positive associations with it (e.g. you've had some great holidays there!)
- Buying on the basis of 'word of mouth' without digging a little deeper and doing your own independent research.
- Most serious of all, buying on a 'hunch' that investing in a certain area will turn out well for you!

There is no substitute for thorough market research before you make any decision. This research should focus on two fundamental questions:

1) "How many potential tenants are there in this area?" And, if there is sufficient demand:
2) "Does the amount that I can charge potential tenants represent an acceptable return on investment?"

There are many different ways to conduct this research. The following is just some of the basic first steps that you can take:

- If you do not know your potential investment area at all, make sure that you spend some time to familiarise yourself with the physical environment. Spend some time just walking the local streets: you can learn a great deal simply by being an intelligent observer.
- Monitor the rental property ads (newspaper and internet) for your target area over a period of time. Note how many rental properties are being advertised and at what price. 'Track' some of the ads. Ads reappearing week after week can be an indication of a slow rental market and vice versa.
- Discuss the local property climate with some estate agents if possible. It may be worth paying a local expert for this service on a consultancy basis.
- Interact with other landlords in the area. This can be done through attending local events for landlords or through participating in Internet forums.
- Familiarise yourself with local issues. Are there any future developments being planned (e.g. a new university campus, shopping centre, industrial park etc.) that may affect property values and rental returns in the area?
- Obtain detailed reports if available. There are many companies that sell detailed reports on local areas. These reports typically include information not only on property values and rental returns but also on social indicators and trends.

New property investors are sometimes so excited about their

new ventures that they neglect to do the basics. Proper market research is an investment in itself and should be very high on your list of priorities. It is true that it takes a bit of time, and even some money, to do properly but failing to do it will cost you much more in the long run!

# Failing to maintain a balanced portfolio

One of the surest routes to success in the world of investment is to maintain a **balance** between the different types of investments that you hold. The overcautious investor who only invests in the 'sure thing' runs the risk of seeing minimal growth. The compulsive risk-taker, on the other hand, can see his whole investment wiped out by risky investments that turned sour. In the end every successful investment portfolio needs different kinds of investment. This is also true in the world of, albeit with a slightly different perspective.

In the world of the prospective landlord sometimes has to make the choice between properties that deliver good rental incomes against properties that offer the prospect of solid capital growth. Many end up making a choice for one of these options in the early stages of assembling their portfolios and then stick with that decision all the way through. This can be a very costly mistake to make. Having a balanced portfolio can be one of the surest ways to cushion your investments against the inevitable fluctuations in the property market. Let us look at the advantages and disadvantages of each in turn.

**High Capital Growth:** The biggest advantage of investing in high capital growth properties is the fact that it can deliver excellent profits in the long term through the increased value of the property. It should therefore be an essential part of any long term investment strategy. The main disadvantage is the fact that it is generally quite expensive to service the mortgage on these kinds of properties, leaving little or nothing over from any monthly rental income gained on them. This can obviously lead to some serious cash-flow concerns in the short term which can become acute during times of economic downturn when prices are stagnant (or falling) or when the interest rate is rising.

**High Yield:** High yield properties normally generate positive cash flows for the investor. This will enable the investor to be in a better position to 'ride out' a difficult market. It also frees up some cash that can be invested in further property purchases. The main disadvantage is that potential capital growth may be very limited.

Individual needs and investment preferences obviously vary a great deal. All investors should however make sure that they balance their portfolio by including a diverse range of properties in it. Exactly how you strike this balance should be determined by your own specific circumstances. For example, if you are close to retirement you may want to angle your portfolio slightly more towards the high yield side as a means of generating a steady income. If on the other hand, you are just starting out in the world of property, the focus should perhaps be a bit more on capital growth. Whatever you do, however, make sure that you are prepared for the fluctuations of the market by diversifying your investments. The old saying of not having all your eggs in one basket still holds true, even when investing in property!

# Not making use of professional property sourcing

One of the most difficult decisions for any new investor is to decide in which properties to invest. Picking up the local paper or going online to look at all the properties for sale in a given area can be a very daunting experience. Then there is the inevitable 'footwork' that needs to be done before a purchase can be made. Doing searches, telephoning estate agents and the countless viewings... even in spite of all of this hard work investors still tend to make the same basic mistakes: they buy with the heart, they buy too soon, they put in offers that are 'over the odds' etc. The bottom line is this - if you are going to make property your business, you are going to have to approach it in a professional way.

One way of doing this is to get professional help in finding exactly the right property for your investment needs. This is where professional property sourcing companies come in. Making use of their services can not only guide you to the best properties for your purposes, it can also save you a lot of money, as it slims down the chances of paying inflated prices for properties. In fact, some property sourcing companies specialise in assisting buyers to find properties that are currently undervalued.

Some of the services that property sourcing companies can offer are:

- **Inspection and evaluation.** These companies can visit a range of properties on behalf of the investor. The investor can then be supplied with detailed recommendations based on local values, probable rental returns, refurbishment costs, local regeneration projects etc.
- **Advice on buying at auction.** Buying investment properties at auction can sometimes lead to huge savings over the normal market price. A property sourcing company can monitor local and national auctions to check whether properties coming up for sale meet certain of the client's specified criteria. Some of them will even bid on behalf of absent buyers.
- **Advice on buying new-build and off-plan properties.** Most property sourcing companies track local property markets intently and are often aware of new developments and other opportunities before anyone else. This means that they can sometimes assist buyers to obtain brand new properties at a substantial discount.

At first glance it may seem counterintuitive to get someone else to play such a big role in making one of the most important decisions in your life. But it makes perfect sense, when you stop to think about it. Professional property sourcing companies are able to take a much more dispassionate look at the market and can therefore give advice based on solid business reasons, rather than on the basis of personal likes and dislikes. They are, furthermore, very up to date with local issues and market conditions. This means that they have, for the most part, already done some of the 'footwork' that you will have to do if you decide to go it alone.

# Spending too much money on furnishing properties

We all have our own individual ideas on the 'look and feel' of our ideal home. However, one of the biggest traps that new buy-to-let landlords often fall into is to directly apply their own personal tastes to their newly acquired rental properties. Although this may leave the property looking stunning in the eyes of the landlord it may lessen its appeal to the buyer. It may also mean that the property is much more expensive to maintain.

Here are the main reasons why furnishing and decorating according to your own tastes should be avoided:

**Tastes differ!** You may think that your new property looks absolutely stunning. However your choice of furnishings or colour scheme may be the reason why a potential tenant decides not to rent the property. This obviously becomes more of a consideration if your tastes are particularly eclectic or eccentric.

**Simple economics.** The more it costs to put something in the property, the more it will cost to replace. Putting in expensive furniture can put a big dent in your cash flow in the long run.

So how do you steer clear of the temptation to make your new property an extension of your own personality?

- **Try to keep things neutral.** Remember that potential tenants will try to imagine themselves in your property as they are viewing it. You should, therefore, make it easy for them to see how their personal effects (like a favourite rug), are going to fit into your property. This is much easier to do if you stick with neutral colours and furnishings from the outset.
- **Choose durable, low maintenance and easy to replace items.** It is just a fact of life that you will have to repair and/or replace some of the furnishings that you place in your property. This is going to be much easier if you bought the item from your local IKEA than if you bought it on your last trip to Bali! Also, one of the biggest factors as far as 'ease of replacement' is concerned is cost. Avoid hugely expensive initial purchases that can come back to haunt you!
- **Cater for specific needs.** Make sure that you take your target market into account when you furnish your property. For example, if you intend to rent to students, you should make sure that there are desks in all of the rooms.

Perhaps the biggest single issue to consider when furnishing your buy to let property is the fact that these expenses will, in most cases, not be tax deductible. Every single penny that you pay is, therefore, likely to come from your own pocket. Since maintaining a positive cash flow should be one of your highest priorities, this is just another reason why you should be prudent in your furnishing decisions.

## MISTAKE 13

# Trying to figure everything out yourself

It seems that many new property investors have a subconscious image of themselves as 'Lone Rangers', all ready to conquer the big bad world out there. The problem with this self-image is, of course, that it is almost impossible for an individual human being to have all the knowledge and skills to succeed in an area as varied and complex as property.

You may consider it heroic and 'character building' to learn from your mistakes as you go along. The problem is, however, that in the field of investment, mistakes usually come with hefty price tags attached to them. As a businessperson with an eye on the bottom line you should, therefore, do your absolute best to avoid mistakes rather than thinking they are interesting learning opportunities!

As we have already seen, you should seriously consider assembling a panel of experts who can form the 'support team' for your investment venture. You should at the very least seek out, and pay careful attention to, the advice of the following people:

• **Bank manager/mortgage advisor.** Money makes the world,

and indeed your business, go round. You should be absolutely sure that you make monetary decisions in an informed way. This is especially true with regards to the level of financing that you can obtain for your purchases. It is obviously very advantageous to have this information available **before** you make any commitments, but sadly many investors miss even this basic step. Liaising with the personnel at your financial institution before you start the property sourcing process will give you much more confidence, as well as bargaining power, throughout the process.

- **Accountant.** Financial management and reporting is an absolute necessity in all businesses and there is no exception. Unless you are a trained accountant yourself you will need someone to help you with this. If you are serious about running your business, 'back of the envelope' calculations will not suffice. If you have a good accountant you can make your decisions based on accurate, up to date, information and will be better able to report on the state of your business when so required.

- **Tax advisor.** Tax law is a complex, constantly changing, field. You can save yourself a great deal of money by ensuring that you get the best, and most up to date, tax advice.

- **Solicitor.** As a landlord and an investor you will be signing quite a few legal contracts and at some point you may have to take legal action. It is therefore in your best interests to build a relationship with a legal professional who you can trust to advise and represent you when needed.

- **Seasoned pro/mentor.** You will gain a significant advantage by finding, and spending time with, someone who has been around the block a few times. If you must learn from mistakes it is always better to learn from someone else's!

You may like the image of the Lone Ranger riding into the

sunset, satisfied with the fact that he succeeded by his own efforts. Just remember, however, that the 'West was won' not by applying quick fixes (important though they seemed at the time) but by people who stuck together to build something for the greater good!

The bottom line: You need a team around you that you can call upon as and when it's necessary.

# Not offsetting legitimate expenses against tax

Most investors know from the outset that their rental income will be liable to income tax. What few realise, however, is that it is possible significantly to reduce what they pay in income tax by offsetting a variety of legitimate expenses against their annual tax bill. Tax is a complex field and you should always seek professional advice on your specific circumstances. However, here are a few general principles before we look at some of the specifics of reducing your tax bill.

- Inland Revenue does not look at the income from your property in isolation. Your income from this source will go into the 'pot' of your total income as far as your tax return is concerned. You should therefore make sure that your tax planning is optimised for your total income rather than for just this one revenue stream.

- If your property portfolio is your only source of income you should take your personal tax allowance into account in your tax planning, as you only pay tax on the amount over and above your personal allowance. This will probably not make a huge difference to your bottom line but every little bit helps!

- If you make a loss in a given year it is sometimes possible to carry that loss over into the next tax year and then to offset it against future profits.

There are also some specific expenses that you can offset against your tax bill. Again, you will need to consult your own tax advisor but what follows is a rough guide to the kind of expenses that you can claim for:

- Council tax and rates
- Insurance premiums directly related to your properties
- Utility service bills (e.g. gas, electricity, water)
- Maintenance and repairs
- Finance charges
- Expenses related to lease renewals
- Legal and consulting fees (excluding the cost of setting up the lease)
- Estate or letting agent's fees
- Travel to and from the property for legitimate business reasons
- Stationary and postage
- Telephone and other communication costs

While the above list may sound like music to the ears of any investor you should also realise that there are certain expenses that you cannot offset against your tax bill. These include:

- Personal expenses (for example, you cannot claim the time that you spend running the business as a legitimate expense)
- Capital expenditure in acquiring new properties
- Capital expenses related to the upgrading of properties
- Furnishing the property
- The legal cost of drawing up the lease

It should be clear from the above that a great deal of money could be saved by consistently offsetting all allowable expenses against tax. As a new investor you should grab this opportunity to improve the financial footing of your business with both hands!

# Not having systems in place to reduce Capital Gains Tax liability

Capital Gains Tax (CGT) has the nasty habit of sneaking up on property investors when the time comes to sell their properties. It is therefore prudent to take some early steps to reduce your CGT liabilities from the outset. For your purposes as a landlord, Capital Gains Tax can simply be defined as a tax payable on the **profits** from the sale of a property that is not your primary residence. In the past this tax was levied on a tiered basis, but in the 2008 budget it was announced that it will henceforth be levied at a flat rate of 18% after the deduction of a £9,600 personal CGT allowance.

As an investor it is obviously very much in your interest to decrease your potential CGT bills as far as possible. There are several ways to do this, some of which are straightforward. Please keep in mind that tax law can be very complex and that it is constantly changing. The following should therefore be seen as general guidelines and not specific advice:

- You can, if at all possible, live in one of your investment properties for a period of time (months rather than weeks!). This can lead to the property being deemed as your principal residence and therefore being exempt from CGT.

- Consider joint ownership of investment properties with your spouse or partner. This will, at a stroke, double the CGT personal allowance threshold above which tax becomes payable.

- Capital expenditure and/or improvements can be claimed against the final CGT bill (as long as you have not previously offset these expenses against income tax).

- You can also offset professional fees related to your purchase and management of a property against your CGT bill. These can include charges made by solicitors, surveyors, financial advisors and mortgage specialists. (Again you should not have previously claimed these fees as expenses against income tax.)

- HM Revenue introduced a new system called 'Entrepreneur's Relief' on 6 April 2008. Under this system the first £1 million of gains that qualify for relief is charged to CGT at an effective rate of 10%. Gains in excess of £1 million are charged at the normal 18% rate. An individual can make claims for relief on more than one occasion, up to a lifetime total of £1 million of gains qualifying for relief.

- HM Revenue operates a system of 'allowable losses' with regards to CGT. This is quite a complicated area but in essence provides that you can offset losses, not previously claimed against income tax, against CGT under certain specifically defined rules.

- In some cases, especially as your business grows, it may be particularly beneficial to set up limited companies or partnerships in order to decrease your overall tax liability.

CGT can come as a nasty surprise to any investor. Do make sure that you minimise the risk of this happening to you by speaking to your tax advisor about your specific circumstances and by planning ahead.

# Missing the opportunities presented by a slowing market

Slumps in property prices are almost always guaranteed to induce general panic and despondency into the property market. As a smart investor, however, you should realise that there are certain proven ways not only to survive these times of turmoil but actively to profit from them.

It is, for the most part, not very difficult to spot a softening property market. For a start the media will be very keen to tell you about it! As an investor you should train yourself to look beyond the obvious 'doom and gloom' stories in order to gain personal awareness of the current market conditions. This is very important because by its very nature the national media paints with a wide brush. The fact that they work with averages means that there will be a lot of property markets doing much better (and of course, much worse) than the figures that they are reporting. There are a few ways of doing your homework in your own area:

- **Do searches on average sale prices in your area.** This will help you to do your own highly targeted statistical analysis.

- **Monitor the local property ads** (Internet and newspaper) to determine how long individual properties remain on the market. Try to work out the average time that properties remain on the market. Excessive waiting times obviously suggest a tough market.
- **Look out for circumstantial evidence.** Are estate agents going out of business in your area or vice versa? Are developers offering all kinds of 'sweeteners' (more than usual) in order to shift properties?
- **Speak to other trusted investors** about their reading of the market. Pay particular attention to their analysis of local factors and why these factors point to whether economic circumstances will be better, or tougher, in your area.

Having said all this, if you do determine that house prices are indeed sharply falling in your area, there is no need to panic. It is possible to profit from a depressed market if you can manage to position yourself correctly:

- Use the media panic to your advantage. Falling house prices are almost always accompanied by tales of 'property Armageddon'. This means that people will sometimes be desperate to get rid of properties that they would otherwise have held on to. If you have the necessary funds you can therefore use this phase in the housing cycle to acquire properties at well below their market value.
- Maximise your rental income. Falling house prices need not be bad news for buy to let investors. Rental demand almost always increases during times of downturn, since people tend to offload properties or postpone buying decisions. The basic laws of supply and demand mean that you can, therefore, work towards higher occupation at better rental rates.

It is very easy to be dragged down with the general negativity that comes with a slowing property market. However, being led into despondency might just mean that you miss out on striking some of the best deals, and enjoying some of the best rates of rental return, from your career.

# Failing to understand the difference between property investment and property speculation

Many people get their ideas about investing in property from dinner party or pub conversations, which tend to focus on how someone made vast sums of money by buying and quickly reselling property. They then tend to shy away from the whole area since they, erroneously, think that you need to have nerves of steel and a very large amount of capital to get involved in property. This is rather unfortunate, since what they have been hearing should properly be defined as **property speculation** rather than property investment.

The dictionary definition of the verb to **speculate** is: "…to engage in any business transaction involving considerable risk or the chance of large gains, esp. to buy and sell commodities, stocks, etc., in the expectation of a quick or very large profit." Applied to the world of property, speculation has the following characteristics:

- Speculators focus on buying undervalued properties and then very quickly offloading them again at a profit (sometimes after renovating or 'adding value' to them in some way).

- It is an activity best undertaken on a full time basis since it requires a great deal of specialised knowledge.
- It requires a large amount of operating capital and people who engage in it are not usually dependant on the rental incomes from the properties they buy. It is short term and high risk.
- Property speculation tends to be a feature of rapidly expanding markets when it is used by people with ready access to capital to profit from rising prices. This does not mean that speculators are not active in times of market downturn. It just takes a lot more skill to profit from such markets and it therefore only attracts the 'hardcore' speculators!

Property speculation is a world away from regular investment and the two should not be confused. Property investment is fundamentally different in the following ways:

- Responsible property investors work with a long-term strategy in mind. The risks involved are also significantly lower than is the case of speculation. This is because long term focuses on steady capital growth underpinned by rental income (which is often used as a source for further expansion).
- Since a good strategy takes the 'long view' it is much better able to withstand different market conditions, whereas most speculation tends to occur during times of rising prices.
- Long-term does not require the same huge capital outlay and cash-flow needed for effective property speculation. It is therefore an area that is much more accessible to the 'ordinary' investor.

It is sometimes possible to make a 'quick buck' from property. In the long-term, however, it is a much more solid strategy for the ordinary investor to focus on the 'slow buck'! This can be achieved through a responsible investment strategy focused on solid rental returns and long term capital growth.

# Failing to realise the benefits of commercial property

When most people think about property investment, they automatically think of a landlord who owns several residential properties. It is true that a good income and solid investment growth can be achieved through investing solely in residential property. However through either fear or ignorance many investors miss out on the huge opportunities of another, potentially very lucrative, market: **Commercial Property.**

As the term indicates Commercial focuses on investment in properties in which business is conducted. As with any kind of investment it is absolutely imperative that you conduct solid market research before you invest in this area. There are, however, several advantages in doing so:

- If you can manage to obtain a property in an in-demand commercial area you will be more or less assured of your property being continuously tenanted. Unlike some residential tenants, companies tend not to relocate at the drop of a hat. This means that commercial property can provide you with a much more stable income stream. Lease terms are often signed for as long as 5 years or even 10 years.

- In the UK the responsibility of repairing and insuring a commercial property usually rests with the tenant. The tenant is also responsible for all utility and rates bills. This means that managing a commercial property is often less labour intensive than is the case of residential properties.
- Commercial property is an ideal investment vehicle for investors who are satisfied with slow, but steady, capital growth and who require a reliable income stream.
- Commercial property leases include regular rent reviews. If a business is successful in a particular area the landlord can use this fact as leverage during rent reviews to press for increased rents. A successful business would be much less likely to move due to a rent increase than a residential tenant, which allows much more scope for negotiation.
- There are some distinct tax advantages in investing in commercial properties. It is even possible to incorporate part of a commercial property portfolio into a personal pension plan. A professional tax advisor will be able to provide more information on the different options open to you.

No area of potential investment is without its risks. The commercial market is, like the residential market, vulnerable to changes in the economic climate. Usually it also takes longer to sell a commercial property. It is therefore imperative that you do everything in your power to understand the local market before you invest in commercial property. As a general rule of thumb, it is always better for the first time commercial investor to invest in an established commercial district with high occupancy rates and proven 'footfall'. It is true that these markets are harder to enter due to higher initial capital costs, but such an investment could prove to be considerably beneficial in the long run.

# Not understanding and applying the principle of 'gearing'

Property investment is unique in the sense that banks and other financial institutions will lend you the money to fund your investment. This means that, unlike investing in shares, you can actually use other people's money to build up your assets. This process is called 'gearing' and it simply means that you use an initial investment to take control, with the help of a financial institution, of an asset with a much greater value than the funds available at your disposal.

To use a simple illustration: if you have £20 000 at your disposal you can use it as a deposit on a property worth £200 000. The rest of the funds can be obtained from the bank in the form of a mortgage. As this property grows in value your gain will be on the capital growth of the full £200 000 rather than merely on the £20 000 that you invested initially. Gearing is therefore a strategy to invest your money in such a way that it can work in conjunction with 'other people's money' to earn you the maximum possible profit. Investors often distinguish between 'high' and 'low' gearing. 'High' gearing refers to instances where only a small percentage of the investor's own funds are invested and vice versa.

It is essential that when you approach you have a clear understanding of the power of gearing. It would be foolish to use just your own funds to invest in property. In fact, you would perhaps be better off investing it in stocks or shares. Gearing, however, gives you the opportunity to get 'partners' (also known as banks!) with serious financial clout on board. In the long run, gearing can also have a compounding effect as capital growth from geared properties allows you to put down deposits on new properties. This can create a kind of snowball effect if it is managed correctly.

Gearing obviously works very much in the investor's favour during times of house price growth since it is much easier to realise capital growth. This does not mean, however, that you should not use the principle of gearing to your advantage during times of economic downturn. During such times it would perhaps be better to use 'Low gearing' (i.e. investing more of your own money). In fact the banks will probably force you to do so by limiting the amount that they are willing to lend to you. If you do your homework properly, this can mean that you use your capital to obtain control of properties that may currently be seriously undervalued. You can, in future, when the market goes through a growth phase revert to higher gearing by re-mortgaging the property and using the cash generated for additional purchases.

Gearing represents one of the most attractive features of property investment: namely the opportunity to get other people's money working for you. Used responsibly and correctly it can be the bedrock upon which your future prosperity is built.

# MISTAKE 20

# Investing abroad

Many people are confronted with the temptation of buying a property abroad every now and then. This temptation usually comes in the form of a glossy brochure in the newspaper offering amazing rates of return on s in country X or Y. In its most seductive form, it is the sudden thought that invariably enters your head when you visit an exotic location: "Wouldn't it be nice to own a little place here?"

I believe that the temptation of foreign property ownership should, in most cases, be one to resist. Here are some reasons:

- **In most cases you do not know the market into which you are buying.** It is staggering to realise that many foreign purchases are 'impulse buys', decided upon whilst on holiday. This means that people buy property without a thorough consideration of the economic prospects, market conditions and legal framework of the country into which they are buying!

- **Overseas property are sometimes promoted in irresponsible ways.** Greedy property development companies are often engaged in questionable marketing exercises, selling massive amounts of overseas new-built properties with little regard for what the local markets require. This can lead to a glut of properties entering the market and consequently to falling property prices. The current property crisis in the coastal regions of Spain is a textbook example of this.

- **By investing in overseas property you are making yourself vulnerable to local political and legal changes.** It may be that a certain destination is being touted as the ideal place in which to invest at the moment, but who is to say that it will stay that way? A change of government could perhaps bring in an administration with radically different views when it comes to foreign ownership of property. Legislative changes can also wreak havoc on an overseas portfolio. For example, officials in the Indian state of Goa recently changed their interpretation of the law governing foreign property ownership. The result is that many investors are facing the loss of their investment properties.

- **You may, in some cases, struggle to get your money out when the time comes to sell your investments.** Some developing countries operate very strict exchange control systems. This means that, while it is generally easy to bring money into the country, you may have to jump through several very expensive hoops to repatriate your investment returns when the time comes.

This is not to say that you should never, under any circumstances, invest abroad. It is just that you should be extremely cautious and have researched the market very well before doing so. You should, at the very least, take the following steps:

- Consult with a trusted, impartial, local expert who comes highly recommended by other expatriate investors. Obviously your expert should not in any way be connected to the property developer or estate agent with whom you are dealing.

- Do not even think of buying unless it is possible to entrust the management of the property to a very reliable local estate agent.

It is true that there are sometimes great deals to be found in the area of overseas property. It is also, sadly, true that it is an area where many investors get burnt. Do everything in your power to ensure that you are not one of them!

# Paying too much for a property

One of the most difficult things for prospective investors to do is to 'get the hang' of making offers for properties. This means that they can often end up paying more than they needed to. It is interesting to note that purchasing property is one of the few areas in our society where the final price paid is open to negotiation.

It may not be considered normal to go into your local Tesco to haggle about the price of a tin of baked beans, whereas it would be unusual in the case of a property transaction for there not to be some serious negotiation prior to sale. Property purchases are, for most of us, the biggest acquisition that we will ever make. The interesting thing is that some people are very reluctant to take the opportunity to minimise the final price that they will be asked to pay. A huge percentage of property sales are concluded at, or just slightly below, the asking price.

I suppose the main reason for this fact is that some people are simply too embarrassed to make low offers. They somehow seem to think that the seller, and whoever else is party to the details of the offer, will consider them miserly or greedy or worse! The fact is, however, that your portfolio will not be built on the foundations of your pride, or on your efforts to be 'kind' to the other party. In the end it will only happen because of solid and informed business decisions on your part.

Bottom line: If you are not prepared to take part in the cut-and-thrust of sale price negotiation you should rethink your decision to invest in property. Always keep the following in mind:

- It is quite likely that the seller set the asking price with the expectation that there would be some hard negotiations to follow. Simply put, asking prices often contain a lot of 'fat'. By merely offering the asking price, or something slightly below it, you are selling yourself short.
- The individual reasons for wanting to sell a property differ enormously. It may be that a seller is exceptionally keen to sell as quickly as possible and would, therefore, be open to a significantly lower offer. The only way to determine that would be to put in such an offer!
- You should gear your strategy towards a process of three possible offers and counter-offers. Each one of these will move the final amount to somewhere closer to something that is mutually acceptable. If you start from a very high base this will not give you too much space in which to manoeuvre.

It is of course possible that you may still be paying too much in spite of all your hard bargaining. There is one last trick you can put up your sleeve to prevent this. Always make sure that you agree the contracts of sale 'subject to finance approval'. This offers you a degree of protection since the bank will undertake a process of due diligence to determine the value of the property before releasing any funds.

# Not studying the competition

One of the most successful companies in the world is the Microsoft Corporation. It is very interesting to look at how Microsoft got to the dominant position that it currently occupies. The answer may surprise many people. Microsoft excelled at studying the market to see which products had the greatest potential. They would then take that product (operating system, web browser etc.), figure out exactly how it worked and then improve it (arguably) before marketing it as their own. You may have your own views about Microsoft but there is no doubt that this strategy was hugely successful.

So what does the high-tech world of Microsoft have to do with the world of property? Simple: You need to be just as clued up about what the competition is doing! As a landlord you will be in direct competition with several other Buy-to-Let landlords in your local area. Studying their business strategies as well as their successes and failures can, in the long run, give you the competitive edge.

There is of course one big problem with this. While most other Buy-to-Let landlords would be happy to get together with other landlords for a few drinks at the pub, they would not be very keen to 'open the books' to show exactly what they are doing and why. You should therefore be a little creative when attempting to research the competition.

Firstly, find who has the highest rate of occupancy and the highest return on investment. The first part will be fairly easy while the second will probably require a bit of sleuthing on your part.

- You can determine rates of occupancy fairly accurately by keeping a close eye on the local property ads (both in the newspaper and online). If a competitor who owns several properties seldom advertises, it may be that he is very successful at retaining tenants. Ads running for a very short time are probably an indication of a successful method of attracting new tenants.
- Return on investment is obviously a lot harder to determine. However, one almost fool-proof piece of evidence of good returns on investment is a constantly expanding portfolio. Make sure that you are plugged into the local grapevine in order to find out who is buying what!

Once you have a fair idea of who the 'movers and shakers' are in terms of low rates of occupancy (vacancy?) and good rates of return, you should make a concerted effort to study their methods. You can do this by looking at the ways they advertise, doing 'virtual viewings' of their properties on the internet, going to the odd physical viewing and, if circumstances allow this, chatting to them about it! The things that you should pay special attention to are:

- How do they attract and retain tenants? Are they perhaps slightly less picky than you are, or do they follow the opposite strategy of 'aiming high'?
- Do the ways in which they decorate and furnish their properties play a significant part in attracting and retaining tenants?

- How much rent do they charge? Why?
- Have they perhaps been successful in targeting a market that you may not have been aware of?

Consistently asking these questions will perhaps, in time, turn you into one of the successful investors which others want to imitate!

# Not being adequately prepared for the cost and timescale of property improvements

Getting a new property in optimum condition is one of the most important tasks of any prospective landlord. It is obviously much easier to find tenants if you have a neat, well furnished and tastefully decorated property to show to them. In addition to this there are also some legal and statutory requirements that you will have to keep in mind when preparing the property. You need to ensure, amongst other things, that:

- All electrical appliances are safe and adequate for their intended purpose
- All gas installations are safe and comply with appropriate regulations
- The correct smoke detection equipment is fitted
- All outside doors and windows can open properly and can be adequately secured when not in use
- All outside areas, if any, are free from accumulations and excessive vegetation.

You will make your life as a landlord much easier if you obtain a building inspection by a qualified building inspector before the start of the first tenancy. This will show that you have complied with all of the legal and statutory requirements before marketing the property.

Another aspect of getting the property ready is the choice of furnishings and decorating style. It is worth repeating here that you should never attempt to furnish and decorate an investment property as you would your own home. Make sure that, as far as possible, you stay with neutral colours and durable, serviceable furnishings. This will ensure that your property will be a 'blank canvas' onto which prospective tenants can easily project their own style and their own personal tastes.

One thing that always seems to surprise new landlords is the fact that the process of preparing a property in readiness for a tenant move-in invariably requires more money and time than they had originally anticipated. Experienced landlords refer to this as the 'Home Improvement Rule'. It simply states that you have to multiply your first estimate of the cost of getting the property ready to rent by **three times the money** and **twice the time**! This fact can obviously come as quite a shock to anyone not prepared for the expenditure and extra time that will be required.

As a new landlord you should ensure that you factor the 'Home Improvement Rule' into all your calculations. This is especially important when calculating the financial implications of renting a new property. You should:

- Ensure that your cash-flow is healthy enough to cope with the demands of preparing the property.
- Allow for the fact that you will not be receiving any rent while the property is being renovated. You should therefore set aside adequate funds to pay the mortgage during this period.

Getting a property ready for tenants can often be a very stressful experience for new investors. It need not be that way. Just make sure that you have and maintain a realistic view of what to expect (both in terms of time and money) and prepare accordingly!

# Attempting to operate without sufficient cash reserves

Your property business, like any other business, cannot succeed unless you have sufficient cash flow to support operating expenditure.

It is obvious that is not just about buying a property and then sitting back to enjoy the proceeds. There are several areas which require frequent expenditure in order to ensure the long-term success of the business. These include:

- Preparing properties for rental
- Repairs
- Legal and accounting fees
- Consulting fees
- Marketing

All of the above cost money so you need to ensure that you can pay for it! If you do not have a positive cash-flow you will almost inevitably be forced into making bad decisions. Decisions such as:

- Doing repairs 'on the cheap' because you cannot afford proper standards of material or workmanship.

- Accepting tenants who you would normally not allow anywhere near your property because you need the rent that they will (hopefully!) pay.
- Giving in to all kinds of excessive demands from tenants because you have a mortal fear of losing them and ending up with a vacancy that you can ill afford.
- In the most extreme cases the stress associated with the lack of a positive cash flow can cause people to sell their properties and abandon the world of altogether.

In short, when you have no cash reserves you act irrationally and in a way that will be detrimental to the long-term health of your business. If you do have sufficient reserves the opposite applies. In this case you can:

- Hold out for better rental rates
- Pass up on less qualified tenants
- Be in a position to not be intimidated by threats to leave from tenants if you do not meet certain demands
- Repair and maintain your properties to the highest possible standard

It is probably one thing to say that a positive cash-flow is very important when running a property business, but acquiring and maintaining a positive cash-flow is a different matter altogether. However, there are a few basic things that you can do:

- Consider delaying the purchase of your first property until you have enough money in reserve to cover any eventualities during the first few months.
- Set aside a percentage of all rental income to go into an operating account from which you can pay normal business expenses
- Consider setting aside some money as a contingency fund from which you can cover unexpected expenses and repairs.

- Use the sale of a property as an opportunity to boost your cash-flow by depositing some of the profit in your operating account.

It is not that difficult, under certain market conditions, to enter the world of property without huge initial investments. What is very difficult, however, is to attempt to run a business without sufficient reserves of cash to cover operating expenses. You should therefore ensure that you have proper cash-flow strategies in place even before you make your first investment.

# Being underinsured

When you stop to think about it, there are lots of things that could go wrong with your business. These range from the cataclysmic (one of your buildings being destroyed by fire or flood) to the more 'run of the mill' (tenants failing to pay up). In light of this it is imperative that you acquire the best possible insurance to protect you from both the big, and - as far as possible - the small, challenges to the health of your business.

Many new landlords do not realise that there are special insurance products, specifically developed for landlords, on the market. They therefore try to cobble together an insurance package as best as they can. This approach leaves many landlords massively underinsured, which can lead to great hardship and even the end of some businesses.

There is no reason why any property business should fail because of insufficient insurance. The growth in buy to let investments did not go unnoticed by the UK insurance industry and a number of landlord insurance packages have come onto the market during the past few years. These policies are designed to address some of the contingencies faced by landlords. Policies can differ quite substantially, but the following is a rough guide to the kind of things that can be covered under landlord insurance:

- Material loss or damage to buildings and/or contents
- Cover for the costs of alternative accommodation for a tenant following insured damage to a property
- Cover for the loss of rent (usually for up to 12 months) following insured damage to a property.
- Property Owners' Liability
- Employers' Liability Indemnity. This covers possible incidents involving cleaners, gardeners, caretakers, and persons doing minor maintenance and repairs.
- Cover between lets for unoccupied properties
- Some policies offer a 'rent guarantee insurance'. This is intended to cover you against loss of rent caused by tenants defaulting on payments. Policies like this will normally cover the rent payment for a short period, usually for the time that it takes to recover possession of the property.

It should be clear from the above that taking out proper landlord insurance can significantly shield you against events that can adversely affect your business. There are, however, some important considerations to take into account before 'signing on the dotted line':

- Do not automatically accept the first quotation that you receive. Significant savings can be made by shopping around.
- The price of the policy should not be the only consideration. You should also check the extent of the cover and possible exclusions when comparing policies.
- You should attempt to strike the balance between adequate cover for what you need and not paying for things that you do not require. You may need professional help with this.

- Make sure that you understand the policy in full before signing. Consult your solicitor if necessary.

Just imagine how it must feel to lose your business because you did not properly prepare for contingencies. Taking out adequate insurance is one way of ensuring that you never have to know how that feels!

# MISTAKE 26

# Not understanding the principles of effective tenancy management

You may think that your decision to invest in property is all about understanding some basic business principles and managing the financial side of your growing property portfolio. It is indeed about both these things. There is, however, another aspect to that very often comes as a shock to new investors: dealing with people! Becoming a property investor will, by definition, include having to deal on a regular basis with the people who live in your properties. Familiarising yourself with the basic principles of tenancy management can, therefore, make your life as a landlord much easier and also prepare you for the inevitable 'tricky' situations that will arise.

At its most basic, the goal of effective tenancy management is to get the best possible tenants (i.e. people who pay on time, look after the property well and do not make excessive demands) and then to get them to stay for as long as possible. The flip side of this coin is that you should also have systems in place to get rid of problem tenants as quickly as possible!

The following are some of the most important things that you should implement as part of an effective tenancy management plan:

- **Make sure that you have the maximum degree of legal protection permitted under the law.** The legal contracts that you sign with tenants should be drawn up in such a way as to allow you to remove unsuitable tenants as efficiently as possible if the need arises. It is therefore important that you do not use 'cookie cutter' contracts but that you discuss your specific needs with a solicitor who can help you design the best possible contracts for your circumstances.

- **Draw up a comprehensive application form.** After the contract, the application form will be the most important 'paper tool' that you can use in the tenancy management process. A good application form ensures that you have some of the prospective tenants' intentions, and also their understanding of the terms of the contract, on paper. This document can later, if necessary, be used as the basis for a repossession process if it can be proven that the tenant knowingly made a false statement in it.

- **Screen tenants carefully.** Always remember that it is better to keep a property vacant for a short time than to allow a problem tenant into your life! You should therefore take care not to make hasty decisions when selecting tenants. Always ask for references and then consistently follow them up. In addition to this, credit checks should also be done on all prospective tenants.

- **Conduct an entry interview (if possible).** First impressions are often lasting. You should, therefore, from the outset make it clear to your tenant that you will deal with them in a professional way, but that you will also not tolerate behaviour not in your best business interests.

- **Provide a good inventory.** A comprehensive inventory is worth its weight in gold as it can be used very effectively as protection against losses caused by tenants.

- **Deal promptly with tenant enquiries and complaints.** You should ensure that you develop a reputation for prompt and decisive action whenever there is a problem or when a repair is needed. Not doing so may just give your tenants an excuse for not paying the rent!
- **Have good systems in place for collecting rent and for dealing with non-payment.** Your rental income is the lifeblood of your business. You should therefore take every possible measure to protect it and to streamline its collection.

Bear in mind that these points only outline the bare bones of an effective tenancy management system. Make sure that you familiarise yourself with the concept and that you also train yourself in its application.

# Not factoring in the potential Capital Gains Tax implications of re-mortgaging

A central plank in the growth strategy of many buy to let investors is to re-mortgage their existing properties in order to release equity to fund further purchases. This is an inherently sound strategy on which many successful portfolios have been built. There is however, one factor that is very often not taken into account: The Capital Gains Tax (CGT) implications of re-mortgaging.

Capital Gains Tax is a tax levied on the **profit** from the sale of a property. It does not enter the equation when you are re-mortgaging since you are not selling the property. This does not mean that you should not take cognisance of it though, since withdrawing equity from a property can seriously affect your ability to pay your CGT bill when you eventually decide to sell it. The crux of the problem is that Capital Gains Tax is based on the difference between sale proceeds and purchase cost. You calculate CGT liability by deducting the original cost of your property from what you eventually sold it for. What you do not deduct is the outstanding amount of your mortgage on the property. This means that if your additional borrowings (generated by re-mortgaging) have been spent or used to expand your portfolio you will have liability to the lender without a corresponding deduction in your CGT calculation. In simple terms you can end up owing more (to the financial institution and the taxman) on the property than it is actually worth.

The above scenario is especially prevalent in situations where properties that have shown excellent capital growth have been very heavily re-mortgaged. Take a look at the following, obviously hypothetical, illustration: Peter buys a property in 1995 for £25,000. Over the years he consistently re-mortgages it to 85% of its (growing) value. When he decides to sell his property in 2025 it is worth £360,000 and he owes £306,000 on it. This means that he nets £54,000 on the sale after paying back the bank. This may sound impressive until the taxman comes knocking. The Revenue will calculate his profit on the sale as £335,000 (£360,000 minus the original price of £25,000) and tax him accordingly. At current rates (and assuming that he used his annual exemption elsewhere) his CGT bill will be around £80,000. This means that he will actually be out of pocket to the tune of £25,000 when selling the property!

Getting out of this trap will be very difficult since you have basically only three options

1) Absorbing the losses - obviously not very palatable
2) Hanging on to the property - this can leave you with the nightmare situation of not being able to afford the property while, in some cases, also not being able to afford to sell it!
3) Emigration - If you live outside the UK for five years you are not liable for CGT.

If none of the options listed above seem particularly attractive you should ensure that you do not end up in such a situation in the first place. Seek professional tax and financial advice before re-mortgaging. Your advisors will be able to advise you on the levels to which you can re-mortgage while still being able to pay your CGT bills from the eventual sale proceeds. This so-called 'safe haven' level could, in time, provide just that!

# Keeping underperforming properties in your portfolio

As your portfolio grows it becomes ever more important to monitor the relative performance of your properties. This is a habit that you should get into, especially since it is very difficult to have the 'vital statistics' of more than a handful of properties at your fingertips.

A good way of monitoring your portfolio's performance is to list all your properties on a spreadsheet and to create a graph showing the following values for all your properties:

- Actual rental income
- Rental income as a percentage of mortgage repayment
- Estimated capital growth
- Occupancy rates
- Total expenditure: agent's fees (if any), marketing costs, legal fees, repairs etc.
- Repairs/maintenance as a percentage of total expenditure
- Total 'cost' of vacancies (mortgage repayments, rates and utilities, insurance etc.)
- Total return on investment (Calculating this can obviously be quite complicated but should be a useful exercise nonetheless)

If you maintain these figures they will very quickly show up the 'stars' and the 'duds' in your portfolio. All of this may be very interesting to you, but the object should not just be to perform an enlightening intellectual exercise. The big question should be what you are going to do with the information that you have gained. The answer should be obvious: you should get rid of the underperforming properties as quickly as possible!

Getting rid of properties seems almost counterintuitive to new property investors. For most of them the default image is that of an ever-expanding portfolio. While this may be true for the most part, it is senseless to hang on to properties if they are losing you money on a daily basis!

Another reason for the reluctance among some investors to sell underperforming properties is the strong emotional attachment that they often develop to them. Some investors will tell you that selling one of their first investment properties would almost break their hearts. The answer to this problem is a maxim that property investors need to repeat to themselves on a regular basis: Your business is a **business** first and foremost. When you are making buying and selling decisions with your heart, the alarm bells should be ringing.

Upon selling your underperforming properties you should, of course, make sure that you replace them as soon as possible, but with what? Well, if you kept an analysis of your portfolio you already have the answer! Try to determine what your best performing properties have in common (location, target market etc.) and then do everything to replicate that formula with your new investment. If you do this you will soon have a portfolio that is constantly evolving and working harder for you - not the other way around!

# Not diversifying risk

Significant wisdom can be gained from old sayings. Our favourite "Do not put all your eggs in one basket" translated into business terminology, speaks now of the need to diversify risk as far as possible. This means that you should structure your portfolio in such a way that poor performance in one market segment or one geographical area does not spell the end of your business.

Although it is tempting simply to 'stick with what you know' when you are investing in property, this could prove disastrous as a strategy in the long term. As your property portfolio grows you should aim to diversify in the following directions:

- **Geographical area:** Having all of your properties in the same suburb of the same town or city is never a good idea as it will make you extremely vulnerable to economic shifts within that area. For example, many landlords who are heavily invested in small geographical areas can attest to the damage done to their property portfolios when large local employers lay off part of their workforce.

- **Tenant type:** Target your portfolio towards different types of tenants. You can, for example, cushion yourself against the big seasonal shifts in incomes that come with housing students by also having properties aimed at more stable, professional tenants.

- **Property type:** Having many different types of properties is another excellent way to protect yourself against the fluctuations in the economy. Having only large 'top of the line' properties aimed at professional tenants can hit you hard during times of recession. If, however, you also have some smaller properties on your books it will mean that you can offer something to people who are 'downshifting' because they are feeling the pinch of the economy.

- **Market segment:** Most landlords immediately think in terms of residential property when they start to plan their investment portfolios. This means that they often miss out on some of the excellent opportunities offered by the commercial property market. Investing in commercial property may seem slightly daunting at first, but the fact is that commercial properties can offer investors stable income streams, long term tenants and steady long term capital growth. My advice to all investors would therefore be to consider branching out into commercial property at some stage.

It is true that acquiring and managing a diversified property portfolio will require significantly more work in the short term. However the payoff will be that it will leave you much better insulated against the inevitable ups and downs that are a feature of the economy in general and the property market in particular.

# Unquestioningly trusting your solicitor with your funds

As a landlord you are going to have to deal with solicitors on a regular basis especially when buying and selling properties. One of the crucial skills that you will have to develop early on is to manage your relationship with your solicitor in such a way that it works to your benefit and not merely the other way around.

One of the key things that you need to realise is that it is often the case that money 'gets lost' in solicitors accounts during property transactions. This is mostly due to inefficient systems of financial management but it is sadly sometimes also caused by what can be generously termed 'wilful neglect' on the part of the solicitor. To counteract this you should keep extremely close tabs on any funds deposited with a solicitor, and make sure that any balance due to you at the end of a transaction, or multiple transactions, is indeed paid out.

A few quick tips for managing your relationship with your solicitor:

- **Carefully scrutinise every statement or piece of correspondence that you receive.** Whenever you receive correspondence or financial statements from your solicitor you should take care to go through it with a fine toothed comb! This will not only help you to determine the exact fee structure applicable to the transactions that you are entering into, but will also help you to be continually aware of the amount of money lodged with the solicitor and the timing and circumstances of its payment to another party, or to you. You should also make sure that you read, and understand, all the terms and conditions and 'fine print' contained in correspondence from your solicitor. This can help prevent some 'nasty surprises' later on!

- **Get every bit of communication confirmed in writing.** There is an old saying that a verbal agreement is not worth the paper it is written on! You should always keep this in mind when you are dealing with solicitors. Whenever there is a dispute one of the primary ways of resolving it is to follow the paper trail. Therefore, if you do not have a proper record of events and correspondence you cannot expect a dispute to be resolved in your favour. You should therefore file every letter to and from your solicitor in a safe place. Furthermore, you should follow up every phone conversation with your solicitor by sending him/her a short written summary of what you understand the outcomes of the meeting or conversation to be. If you use e-mail for communication, make sure that you request a 'read receipt' with every message you send to your solicitors' office.

- **Work on a long term business relationship.** It will probably take a bit of 'trial and error', but you should eventually work towards finding a solicitor with whom you feel you can work over the long term, and then channel most of your business in their direction. The basic laws of economics dictate that you will probably get a better service from such a relationship, since losing you as a regular client will almost certainly impact upon the law firm's 'bottom line'.

# Not understanding that the vendor needs you more that you need him

As a property investor you should remember that, in some ways, you are negotiating from a position of strength when buying a property. As a buyer you have the option of purchasing any of a number of properties in your price range and/or target market. The seller, on the other hand, is trying to sell one particular property. You should always use this fact to your advantage. Here are some ways in which you can do this:

- **Do not allow yourself to be pressured into premature buying decisions.** Sellers and their agents will often use a variety of 'hard sell' techniques in order to get you to sign on the dotted line as quickly as possible. This will sometimes include warnings that someone else will snap up the property if you do not act within the next day or so. You should train yourself to see this kind of pressure for exactly what it is: a sales technique! Keep a cool head and do not make any hasty decisions. The only exception to this should be when you are absolutely convinced, after conferring with some trusted advisors, that you are indeed faced with a 'once in a lifetime' opportunity. The fact is, however, that losing out on buying most properties, while inconvenient, would not be a major disaster. In fact, you will lose more from making hasty decisions than the other way around.

- **Take time to do proper research and 'due diligence'.** So if you are not supposed to make hasty decisions, how should you use the time that you have gained? The answer to this question should be obvious. If you are not rushed into making decisions it means that you have a lot more time to investigate the property in which you are interested, and come to a decision about whether it is a sound investment and therefore a worthy addition to your portfolio. Some of the questions that you will need to answer before putting forward an offer include: What is the rental demand in the area that I am considering? Does the level of rent that I can likely charge represent a good return on investment? What is the likely cost of getting the property ready for tenants to move in? Are there any 'on the ground' factors in favour (or against) the property? Are there any long-term factors (new developments, demographic changes etc.) that should be taken into account?

It should be clear from the above that buying a new property is something that is best done in a 'slow and steady' way. In fact, 'snapping up' properties because you were advised that they would very likely be sold in a flash, is a sure way to getting egg on your face. The easiest way to avoid doing this is to remind yourself on a continual basis that you are holding the best cards.

# Forgetting that the estate agent is NOT your friend

For every property that you are interested in you are likely to deal with several estate agents. It is therefore imperative that you develop a solid understanding of the role of estate agents and also a strategy for dealing with their sales techniques.

Perhaps most importantly you must remember that the estate agent is acting on behalf of the seller, and that he gets paid a certain percentage of commission on every sale that he facilitates. It is therefore in the interest of the agent to

a) Make sure that the property sells at the best possible price (the higher the sale price the higher their commission)
b) Get the sale through as quickly as possible (agents normally do not get paid until the sale is finalised) and
c) Serve the best interests of the seller (an agent who gets the reputation of not 'delivering' for sellers will soon be out of business). This means, in summary, that an agent approaches all possible buyers with the intention of attempting to sell properties to them at the highest price possible in the shortest time possible.

It is often the case that agents will try to underplay the factors mentioned above and try to pass themselves off as a 'friend to the buyer'. As a potential buyer you should not be hoodwinked by this. The basic laws of economics dictate that agents cannot consistently act in ways that are detrimental to the interests of sellers. You should therefore be on the lookout for the following:

- Agents will often exaggerate the potential return on investment of a particular property by emphasising its 'amazing' rental potential. It may indeed be the case that a property will do very well on the rental market. You should not, however, make a decision about this fact purely on the advice of an agent.

- Agents often 'talk up' the relative popularity of a property, urging you to 'snap it up' before someone else does. In cases like this you should always remember that 'there are many fish in the sea' even in the property world! As a buyer you are therefore negotiating from a position of strength.

- Agents are aware of the fact that many people buy with the heart rather than with the head. This means that you will sometimes be faced with appeals to your emotions while deciding whether or not to invest in a property. You should, therefore, constantly remind yourself that you are running a business and that emotions should not enter into the decision making process at all.

- Agents will sometimes indicate that they would be willing to negotiate a 'special price' with the seller. This is almost always an indication that the agent thinks that the property might be overpriced rather than a heartfelt attempt to help you get the best deal!

Always remember that your interests and those of the seller's agent are, for the most part, diametrically opposed. This should, at the very least, cause you to take some of the things that you hear from agents with more than just a pinch of salt.

# Forgetting that time is your most important ally while negotiating

In attempting to achieve a quick sale on a property, one of the favourite techniques of sellers and their agents is trying to drum up a sense of urgency in the potential buyer. They do this by pointing out that the particular property is a 'red hot prospect' and buyers are almost queuing round the block for a piece of the action! You would do very well to disregard this kind of 'sales talk' completely. As an investor, your most important ally and asset is **time**:

a) Time to weigh up your options
b) Time to do your research and
c) Time to work out a realistic proposal based on that research.

Sellers know very well that the opposite of the above is true in their case and that time can often work against them. More time for you means that it is more likely that you would stumble across a defect in the property, a local factor (i.e. rising unemployment) that would make a buying decision less likely, or that you come across another property better suited to your needs. You should, therefore, always regard efforts to rush you into making decisions as a normal hazard of buying property and act accordingly.

So how do you resist the temptation to make snap decisions?

- **Tell the agent that you will not make hasty decisions.** Making it clear from the outset that you are going to make your decisions in a calm and considered way will make it slightly less likely that you will be hassled with 'Act Now!' appeals.
- **Draw up a checklist and work through it.** There is a certain amount of research, and certain things related to due diligence, that you will have to do before making a property purchase. Make a list of these things and only buy a property after you have 'checked every box'. This will force you to take an objective look at the merits (or not!) of the property rather than just being swayed by emotional appeals.
- **Do your homework and get professional advice.** In certain kinds of market conditions it is indeed the case that properties sell extremely fast. This does not mean, however, that you should jump on the bandwagon and make offers at first sight of a property. In conditions like these you would be well advised to do your homework beforehand by getting some professional advice on which properties will be the best investment. You can then enter that market with a clearly defined set of requirements. Having this in hand will make you more or less immune to any efforts to drum up hysteria!

Think for a minute about how many times you have seen a sign proclaiming: 'The deal of the century'. Perhaps once every week or so? This simple fact should cause you to stop and think a bit before giving in to desperate emotional appeals to buy 'before it is too late'.

# Forgetting to factor in costs to get your property ready to let

Property investors often refer to the "Home Improvement Rule". Discussed briefly in Mistake 23, according to this rule it will almost always take **three times the money** and **twice the time** you initially planned to get a property ready to let. As a new investor you should take these figures to heart as it can mean the difference between running a healthy business and coming up against serious cash flow difficulties.

Calculating accurate preparation costs will help you to:

- Ensure that your cash flow is healthy enough to cope with the demands of preparing the property.
- Allow for the fact that you will not be receiving any rent whilst the property is being renovated. You should therefore set aside adequate funds to pay the mortgage during this period.

Having work done on a property is never cheap. There are, however, quite a few ways in which you can keep costs from spiralling out of control:

- **Do some work yourself if possible.** It could be that there are certain tasks that you can undertake yourself at a fraction of the cost that a tradesman would charge you. If you feel confident that you can do the work required you should perhaps take this opportunity to cut costs. Before you do this, however, you should first calculate what your time is worth (i.e. are you not perhaps wasting money by doing plastering while you should be managing your business?) The results of doing this calculation will probably be that you do a lot of work yourself early on, while outsourcing to tradesmen – or women - as your portfolio grows.

- **Shop around.** You should make sure that you get the best possible prices on the materials needed to renovate the property. It is of vital importance to compare the prices offered by different retailers and wholesalers. This can be done very easily by conducting some online research.

- **Get several quotations for each job in the early stages.** If you are using tradesmen, you should initially try not to just stick with the same providers. Give several individuals/firms the opportunity to bid for the work that you want done (and let them all know that they are bidding against other providers). This will ensure that you get work done at competitive rates. Trying out different providers will help you to identify those with whom it would be beneficial to build a long-term relationship.

- **Use contracts to give you the maximum amount of protection.** You should always sign binding contracts with providers before they commence work on big projects (i.e. remodelling a kitchen, doing a loft conversion). Contracts should state clear project milestones and also the completion date (with penalties for late delivery). Having such a contract in place can offer you a degree of protection against the needless dragging out of projects that so often occurs.

Unfortunately many efforts to get properties ready for the rental market are more or less done 'on a wing and a prayer'! You can save yourself a lot of hassle and money by drawing up a very clear plan of what you need to do, when you need it done, and how much it is likely to cost.

# Believing people who tell you that is too risky

There is currently no shortage of doomsayers when it comes to the world of property. Many people take one look at the slump in property prices and conclude from it that getting into property is about as risky as betting your monthly earnings on a horse with a limp! While it is true that no investment is without some element of risk, it should be remembered that buy to let investors can benefit (in different ways) from both strong and weak property markets. Consider the following:

- Rents tend to go down during times of high house price growth. On one level this is bad news for the investor (lower rental yields) but on another level rising house prices translates into excellent long term capital growth.
- Rents tend to go up during times of falling house prices. In this scenario the opposite is true. House price slumps are not great in terms of capital growth but tend to deliver excellent rental yields.

It should be clear from the above that an investor with a balanced portfolio (geared to capital growth **as well as** high rental yields) is in an excellent position to 'ride out' some of the ups and downs of the wider economy.

Furthermore the 'Private Rental Property' market segment is expected to grow to about 20% of the UK property market over the next 15-20 years (against about 11% at the moment). There are many reasons for this projected growth in rental demand. The main ones are the following:

- The UK population is expected to grow by about 5 million over the next two decades. This will be largely due to longer life expectancy and immigration.
- Various restrictions on building new properties means that there will be an increasing shortage of supply (relative to demand) of such properties.
- More and more UK residents are opting to live alone, with the proportion of 'single person households' rising year on year. This fact obviously puts great strain on the housing stock.
- The growth in University enrolment is leading to an increased number of students who require rental accommodation close to their places of study.

The above factors should make it clear to any investor that the 'doom and gloom' of 2008/2009 does not present the whole picture in terms of the property market. Medium to long-term demand for rental properties is likely to be very good. This projected growth in rental demand should, at the very least, encourage the careful investor to give some consideration to getting into the market at the present time.

But this is not a decision to be taken lightly and should only be contemplated with a long-term strategy in mind. The worst thing you can do however is to listen to the doomsayers and then walk away without investigating the possibilities for yourself.

# Not conducting a detailed check-in inspection

As a businessperson one of your top priorities should be to minimise the cost of running your business. One of the things that can add the most 'cost' to your business, both in terms of money spent and time wasted (and 'time is money' after all!), is having to do expensive repairs or replace broken or faulty items after a tenant moves out. One way to minimise the effect of this is to design an effective inventory maintenance strategy. Here are some of the steps that you can follow:

- **Make your inventory as detailed as possible.** Your inventories should leave as little 'wriggle room' as possible in case a dispute arises. It may seem tedious to do so, but you should therefore make sure that your inventory should include just about everything that can get lost, broken or damaged in any way. Do not use 'ball park' descriptions (i.e. drawer full of cutlery) - instead list every single item (6 knives, 6 forks etc.)
- **Review the inventory every time new tenants move in.** Guard against just falling back on the first inventory that you drew up. It may be that you bought something in the meantime or that there was a significant change in the condition of

some of the items listed. Make sure that you reflect this on the inventory.

- **Make sure that the tenants actually sign the inventory.** An unsigned inventory is almost as good as no inventory at all! You should therefore make very sure that the tenants sign the inventory as soon as possible after moving in to the property.

- **Use the inventory as the basis for mid-tenancy checks.** You are well within your rights as a landlord to request an inspection of a property midway through a rental (especially in the case of long leases). Checking the property against the inventory during such an inspection can save you a lot of hassle later on.

- **Use a professional inventory service if needed.** Some landlords do not follow good principles of inventory management simply because they feel that it is too much work! This can indeed be the case if you have quite a few properties on your books, in which case it may be worth your while to engage the services of a professional inventory clerk. Your local business directory can help you to find firms providing this service.

Doing a proper inspection, and producing a proper inventory on the basis of it, can protect you against losses incurred due to negligent conduct on the part of your tenants. Good inventory management is just another example of how doing your homework (and paperwork!) can serve your best interests in the long run!

# Not maintaining a professional landlord-tenant relationship

One of the keys to running a successful property business is the maintenance of a professional relationship with your tenants. At its core, this relationship should be about providing excellent standards of service (within the framework of your statutory responsibilities and the rental agreement) while at the same time expecting the tenant to fulfil his/her obligations. The following are some suggestions for developing a professional landlord/tenant relationship.

- **Try to not to 'get too close' to your tenants.** You may have some wonderful people as tenants but it is always a good idea to maintain a measure of professional distance. Doing rent reviews, or addressing issues of tenant behaviour, can get very awkward if there is a personal friendship that could get in the way.

- **Put everything in writing.** Make sure that you have a 'paper trail' for all your dealings with your tenants. The most important 'piece of paper' governing your relationship with the tenant is obviously the rental agreement. This should be a good quality, easy to understand, contract to which you can easily refer. You should also follow up any verbal communication with tenants (especially about issues like arrears, repairs, complaints by neighbours etc.) with a written summary.

- **Respect tenants privacy.** Tenants have the right to 'quiet enjoyment' of the property that they are renting. Not respecting this can land you in a great deal of trouble in the long run. (You can read more about this issue in the following section.)

- **Fulfil your statutory responsibilities.** You are under a legal obligation to provide safe premises, installations and appliances for your tenants. Not fulfilling this obligation can lead to serious conflict with your tenants, and can also leave you open to the possibility of litigation.

- **Be as accessible as possible.** Make sure that your tenants know how to reach you and respond to any contact from them in a friendly, polite and businesslike manner.

- **Respond quickly to problems and/or complaints.** You should develop a reputation with your tenants as a 'hands-on landlord'. You can develop this by reacting quickly and professionally to requests for repairs, or to any other communication from them. This will leave them with the impression that the property is being actively managed and might make them slightly less likely to default on their rent payments.

- **Handle missed payments according to the letter of the law and in a professional way.** One of the biggest tests for the landlord/tenant relationship is when rent payments are late, or not made at all. The worst possible response in such a case would be to threaten and harass your tenants. This can only serve to sour the relationship and cause you expensive legal problems further down the road. Instead your response should be to find out exactly why a payment is late, or was missed, and then to act strictly within the rights given to you by the law and the rental agreement.

# MISTAKE 38

# Violating tenants' legal rights

Under current UK law it is accepted that tenants have what is called an 'estate in land' in properties that they are renting. This is usually interpreted as having a right to the 'quiet enjoyment' of the property and to treat the property as their own (within the confines of the lease agreement). It also implies that a tenant has the right to privacy in the rental property. This right is currently being interpreted very broadly. As a landlord you should therefore realise that, as far as the right to privacy is concerned, the law is heavily stacked in favour of a tenant.

Not respecting a tenant's right to privacy could land you in legal hot water in the long term as perceived violations of privacy have often been used as the basis for harassment claims against landlords. It would of course be prudent to protect yourself against such claims. The following are some of the ways in which you can do so:

- **Never arrive unannounced and never let yourself into the property without notifying the tenant first.** The only reason to ever make an unannounced entry into a property occupied by tenants should be to deal with a bona fide emergency (e.g. a gas leak). You should in all other cases request entry, in writing, at least 24 hours in advance giving good reasons for doing so.

- **Never change the locks on a property in case of non-payment.** Many landlords have found out the hard way that changing locks while a tenant is still in occupation of a property is never a good idea. It is very likely that you will be sued, and lose the case, if you attempt it.

- **Never threaten the tenant.** This point should perhaps go without saying but it is important to remember that even 'mild' entreaties to pay up, or to take better care in maintaining the property can be construed as threatening behaviour by some tenants. You should therefore do your best to remain calm and professional at all times in your dealings with tenants.

- **Follow the correct legal procedure for evicting tenants.** The laws governing eviction are quite complex. If you have tenants who are in arrears and refusing to pay up, you should get proper legal advice and follow the correct channels. Under no circumstances should you attempt to evict tenants yourself.

- **Carefully document your dealings with unreasonable tenants.** If a tenant makes it extremely difficult for you to do your duties as a landlord (e.g. refusing entry for mid-term checks or safety inspections) it is quite likely that you are going to have some trouble with him/her in the future. In such cases you should carefully document your contact with the person and perhaps even take a witness along to observe when you are refused access after a legitimate and reasonable request. Having solid evidence like this available will greatly strengthen your hand in case of possible litigation.

# Not having the best possible team around you

Beginner investors in property often think they are embarking on a solitary journey. While it is true that you will ultimately have to make the final decisions in your business, you should avoid trying to go it alone at all costs. Trying to do everything yourself will inevitably lead to some bad business decisions, as none of us can be an expert in all the different fields that are relevant to making successful investors. One of your first priorities should therefore be to identify individuals to construct your team:

- **Solicitor** – Every single property transaction that you make will have a legal side to it. Having a solicitor in whom you can trust to act in your best interests can help to ensure that you get the best possible advice and representation.
- **Mortgage Broker** – A good mortgage broker can be worth his/her weight in gold in helping you find the very best deals for your particular circumstances.
- **Accountant** – Running a business without keeping your finances under tight control is asking for trouble. A good, reliable, accountant will not only help you to keep the books

in order but will also serve you well with advice on running the financial side of your business.

- **Letting Agent** – As your portfolio grows it will become an ever greater task to let and manage all the different properties on your books. A competent letting agent can take a lot of this hassle off your mind.
- **Insurance Broker** – One of the biggest mistakes that new property investors make is to be underinsured. Consulting regularly with an insurance broker will ensure that your cover is just right for your circumstances.

So how do you find all of these people? The answer is that you have to work at it; this bit of work will be vitally important to the future success of your business! You should, therefore, from the outset spend time in order to find people who can contribute to your long term success. Here are a few suggestions to help you do just that:

- **Keep your ears close to the ground.** When people receive good service (or bad service for that matter!) they tend to talk about it. You should, therefore, make sure you pay attention when you hear such professionals being discussed.
- **Shop around.** Don't just get stuck with the first people who you work with. It may be that what you initially thought was brilliant service from one person can easily be surpassed. You should therefore move your business around a bit with a view to finding a 'comfortable fit'.
- **Build relationships.** The people on your team should know that you appreciate their efforts and that you are serious about building a long term business with their help. You should strive to maintain excellent relationships with them. Seeing you as a valued, and valuable, long term client will certainly encourage them to 'go the extra mile' for you!

# Not managing your relationship with your solicitor properly

Like it or not, as a property investor you will have to deal with members of the legal profession on a very regular basis. Every contract that you sign will have to be drawn up (or at the very least approved) by a legal professional. Solicitors also play a key role in the transfer of funds between buyers, sellers and financial institutions. This fact means that you should:

- Get a very good solicitor on your team as soon as possible. You should be able to trust your legal representative – almost implicitly - to represent you in the best possible way. Finding such a person may take a bit of time but it is certainly worth the effort.

- Study some of the basic issues relevant to property law. This does not mean that you should strive to become a legal expert. I am simply recommending that you acquire a very good grasp of some fundamental concepts. This will make it so much more difficult for solicitors to hoodwink you into making bad and/or expensive decisions.

- Discuss your specific needs and requirements with your solicitor before every transaction. Some of the biggest legal problems in the property field arise from solicitors applying generic approaches to property deals in which they are involved. You can prevent this happening by detailing your specific requirements in each case. Make sure that you record this communication with your solicitor in writing.

- Make sure that you do not pay over the odds. It is true that legal advice and representation is expensive. You should make sure, however, that you are not required to pay much more than is necessary to your solicitor. You can do this by comparing prices between different firms (you will be amazed at the amount of price variation for standard services) and by investigating whether expensive 'premium services' would actually add any value to the more 'basic' services on offer.

- Check that all your funds are returned to you at the end of a transaction (or series of transactions). As discussed previously, but worth a second mention, money being mislaid is mostly due to inefficient systems of financial management but it is sadly sometimes also caused by what can be generously termed 'wilful neglect' on the part of the solicitor. To counteract this you should keep extremely close tabs on all funds deposited with a solicitor and make sure that any money due to you at the end of a transaction, or multiple transactions, is indeed paid out.

- Do not take out unnecessary indemnity insurance. Your solicitor will sometimes try to convince you to keep on taking out indemnity insurance in order to protect yourself during the transaction. In some cases you will actually be protecting the solicitor and his own indemnity insurance policy! Your solicitor is required by law to have his own indemnity cover in place and shifting the responsibility of taking out cover to you is a handy way for him/her to keep the premiums on that cover down. You should therefore carefully investigate any request to take out cover and refuse if you deem it not to be in your own best interests.

# Not doing correct 'due diligence' when valuing properties

It is a sad fact that many new property investors often engage in the real estate equivalent of 'walking around a car and kicking its tyres' when attempting to value a property! This can be a very costly mistake to make, since trying to assign a value to a property on the basis of a cursory inspection can sometimes be nothing less than an exercise in futility. The fact is, however, that it has never been so easy to get a very accurate idea of the actual worth of a property. This can be done through utilising some of the excellent tools that are being made available to investors on the internet, and as an investor you should, at the very least, look at your proposed properties through the following lenses:

- **Estimates of actual worth.** The best way to get a reliable price estimate is to get a 'real life' surveyor to have a look. If however you want to compare several properties at the same time this can be a very expensive option. In the initial stages of attempting to value a property you would therefore be quite well served by using one of the several online services that offer instant valuations and then instructing a surveyor when you have narrowed your choices.

- **Average property prices and trends in your area.** Unless you are buying a huge, isolated, country estate, the property that you are considering cannot be looked at in isolation. You should therefore make use of one of the online services that allow you to study house price trends in a certain area (or even a certain street). This will give you a good idea of where the market is heading. There are websites that can give you a list of properties for which the asking price was dropped. Having this kind of information at hand could of course be very handy when the time for negotiation rolls around!

- **Environmental Factors.** The property that you are considering may look idyllic, but how will it fare in a flood? The Environment Agency's website allows you to do detailed checks on environmental factors that may affect property prices and/or insurance rates.

- **Social Trends.** As an investor you will want to buy properties in which tenants would feel safe and comfortable. High crime rates would, therefore, make a property less valuable to you. You should make use of the services that offer detailed crime reports, and reports on other social trends, for local areas.

- **Services and Amenities.** Having good schools, transport links and amenities nearby will certainly make a property more desirable to prospective tenants. There are web services available which allow you to examine the availability of such amenities and services in detail.

- **Council Tax and Insurance rates.** It may be the case that the 'gem' that you found is in a very high council tax band, or that it attracts very high insurance premiums. This will obviously make it less attractive and these costs should therefore be researched.

All of the above factors can combine to help you reach a very realistic value of what a property is worth, and how it will likely perform as an investment. Making decisions based on such information can obviously be of huge benefit in the long run.

## MISTAKE 42

# Poor negotiation techniques

As we have previously acknowledged, property is one of the few areas in the economy where the final selling price is open to negotiation, and unfortunately (from the buyer's perspective at least) a very large percentage of homes are sold for an amount quite close to their original asking price. The major reason for this is that buyers either prefer not to negotiate (no way to run a property business of course!), or that they don't have the required negotiation skills when they do.

The following are some tips on sharpening your negotiation skills:

**Start Low**. If you make a relatively high offer from the outset you will be leaving yourself with almost no room to manoeuvre. Your first offer should, therefore, be significantly less than what you would be willing to pay in the end. You should, of course, expect some hard bargaining to follow but at least you have given yourself some leverage by putting in a low offer.

**Never let your true feelings about a property be known**. It may be that you would be willing to move heaven and earth to acquire a certain property (hopefully this is due to solid business reasons and not just emotions!). You would, however, be crazy to show your enthusiasm to the prospective seller. You should do your best to project an attitude of studied indifference when negotiating. This should be maintained at all times, regardless of how much you actually want to own the property.

**Use time to your advantage.** One sure way to show that you are keen to acquire a certain property would be to rush the negotiations. Try to remember that the seller is probably keener to sell than you are to buy and, therefore, you can slow down the process a bit. This will perhaps plant a few seeds of doubt and uncertainty in the seller's mind and make the acceptance of a lower offer more likely.

**Make detailed offers and put them in writing.** You should do your utmost to create the impression that your offer is related to some solid, objective reasons and that you are not merely engaged in a bit of haggling to get the price down. Try to avoid simply making offers over the phone. Instead put your offer in writing and include a detailed breakdown of how you arrived at it. This will let the seller know that you did your homework and that you came to your position after careful thought and analysis.

**Try not to offer 'rounded off' amounts.** This point follows on from the previous paragraph. Offers looking like 'ball park figures' practically beg to be renegotiated since they create the impression that very little thought went into deciding on the final amount.

**Make it known that you would be prepared to 'walk away' under some circumstances.** It is sometimes necessary to call your negotiating partner's bluff and threaten to walk away from the table if you feel that your offers are not being seriously considered. Hinting that you are prepared to quit the negotiations under certain circumstances might go a long way to focusing the seller's mind!

# Not cushioning yourself against difficult times

Another piece of ancient wisdom that you would do very well to heed as a property investor is to always make sure that you "save something for a rainy day ''. Cash flow problems rank very highly among the main reasons for business failures, and nothing exposes a deficient cash flow as quickly and as ruthlessly as a sudden emergency. You should, therefore, always make sure that you develop a 'cushion' in the finances of your business in order to avoid the spectre of a dried-up cash flow rearing its ugly head.

It is obviously not possible to predict every single situation in which you might experience a cash flow problem (hence the term: 'emergencies'!) There are, however, certain times when possible cash flow pressures can be quite accurately predicted. One such time is the period immediately after the acquisition of a new property. This is a time during which properties have to be prepared for new tenants and when those tenants have to be found. The obvious implication of this is that you will be faced with a period during which you will be paying the mortgage on the property while not gaining any income from it. Not being prepared for this can obviously lead to some very stressful situations and can also force you to cut corners with work on the property, or to accept less than ideal tenants into your life.

It should be clear, in light of this, that the creation of a contingency fund should be one of your top priorities after setting up your business. There are several ways in which to create, and manage, such a fund:

- **Consider delaying your initial purchase until you have built up a sufficient 'starter cushion'.** It would be unreasonable to expect that every investor should have a cast iron contingency fund in place before starting out. What you should have in place, however, is a clear assessment of how much money you will need and enough funds (or access to funds) to at least carry you through the first few months. It may, in light of this, be wise to delay an initial purchase until you are reasonably sure that you will be able to survive a bumpy start to your investment career.

- **Continue to set some money aside for your contingency fund.** You should try to set a goal of a certain percentage of rent income to be paid into your 'cushion'. The fund can further be bolstered by also adding a small percentage from the proceeds of sales to it.

- **Have clearly defined protocols in place for when you will make use of the fund.** There should be a clear distinction between your contingency fund and your normal operating account. This distinction can only be effectively made if you clearly define from the outset what would qualify as a 'rainy day' (e.g. not having tenants for a time would qualify; needing cash to go towards 'the deal of the century' would not!)

You may question the wisdom of putting money that could have worked hard for you to one side. However you will find, during an emergency, that this fund could perform one of the most important jobs of all - helping your business to stay afloat!

# Wasting Time

Learn the art of negotiation. There is a fine line between undue haste and efficient speed and it is one that you would do very well to develop. You should not, on the one hand, give the impression that you are absolutely desperate to obtain a property as soon as possible. This will just send the seller a signal to stick with the initial asking price. If, on the other hand, you allow the process to slide either during the negotiation or finalising phase you are setting yourself up for trouble. This is especially relevant in the period before your offer has been accepted since unnecessary delay during this phase could cost you a property that would perhaps have made a worthy addition to your portfolio.

So how do you keep the momentum? The following should be a good start:

- **Make it clear that you have a business to run.** You should do your utmost to convince sellers that the reason why you prefer to move quickly is that you have a business to attend to and that your time is precious. Most people will appreciate that setting and meeting deadlines is an integral part of running a successful business. By stressing the business need for moving the process along you can avoid the perception that you are merely desperate to close the deal.

- **Set a clear timeframe and do your best to keep everyone to it.** You can obviously not force a seller to accept an offer on a specific date. You can, however, state very clearly that an offer would lapse at a certain stage, something which would concentrate the minds of most sellers! Once the offer has been accepted you should set a clear timetable and then strongly encourage everyone on your team - especially your solicitor – diligently to keep to it. Put your requests in writing and then ask for regular status updates. It is indeed sometimes the case that the squeaky wheel gets the most attention!

- **Try to 'hit the ground running'.** The period when a deal is being finalised may sometimes feel as if it is dragging on for ages (although you should do your best to ensure that this is perception and not reality!). This does not mean that you should sit around idly waiting for it to pass. This time should be used to prepare for the completion date so that you can be prepared to get the property ready for tenants as soon as possible. Use it to plan how you are going to furnish the property, do research about how to best advertise the particular property to prospective tenants etc. This will help you to shorten the time between handover of the keys and the first tenants moving in.

We all know the old saying 'time is money'. Nowhere is this truer than in the area of property. Make sure that you heed its message during the purchase of a new property by doing your best to move the process forward towards the time when tenants can move in!

## MISTAKE 45

# Not getting enough information about the condition of a property

Knowing the difference between saving money and an apparent 'saving' which comes back to haunt you is a very important skill to develop. A good example of the latter is when people opt to stick with a basic valuation when buying a new property. This can lead to them to missing some things that would have made them think twice about actually placing their money on the table. I would, in light of this, always recommend that you pay for a Homebuyers Report when considering a purchase.

The main reason for my recommendation is that most of us simply do not know what to look for, especially in terms of possible structural defects, when attempting to assess a property's value. This is where the Homebuyers' Report can be a lifesaver (or should that be a wallet saver?) Unlike the basic valuation, it is carried out for the benefit of the buyer and not for the mortgage lender. It can therefore be used to:

- Ensure that the property is in a good condition
- Evaluate whether you should continue with the purchase at the present price
- Flag up any urgent problems with the property

A surveyor doing the Homebuyers Report will include all the visible parts of the property in their report. They will point out the condition of each area (e.g. the roof, walls etc.) and also whether it needs work done (either straightaway or at a later date). The report will also include recommendations for possible further specialist surveys to be done.

A few practical matters to consider in commissioning a Homebuyers Report:

- The easiest, and often the cheapest, way to obtain a Home-buyers Report is to arrange it with the surveyor who is doing the basic survey on behalf of the mortgage lender. This means that it can then be done at the same time as the basic survey. There is, however, nothing to stop you from finding and instructing your own surveyor.
- The inspection for the report should be done no more than five days after you instructed the surveyor. The actual inspection takes about two hours to complete and you should have the final report within a week. The final report will be fairly detailed (often up to 20 pages) giving you solid information upon which to base further decisions.
- Obtaining a Homebuyers Report will cost you £250 - £500 depending on the value of the property. In my opinion this is money very well spent.

Spending money on a Homebuyers Report can seem like an unnecessary expense at the time but I can assure you it is not. The money spent obtaining the report can mean the difference between acquiring a worthy addition to your property portfolio, or getting a 'lemon' that will give you sleepless nights for years to come!

# Not shopping around
# for the best deals

We human beings are creatures of habit. Unfortunately our habits can sometimes turn out to be very costly. One example of this is when we use a certain shop, person or service just because 'we have always done so!' Just sticking with what you know in this way can cost you a lot of money, as it often means that you are losing out on better deals elsewhere. I probably do not have to tell you that keeping your costs down is one of the most important things you need to do in managing an effective business. 'Shopping around' should become a regular habit.

Allow me to make a brief remark about service before we dive into the practicalities of finding the best deals. It may sometimes be the case that you are receiving excellent service from a provider (i.e. a solicitor, mortgage broker etc.) while being aware that you are paying slightly more than the going rate for it. In such cases you should carefully weigh your options. It would be very foolish to forego a level of service that you would be hard pressed to find anywhere else just in order to save a few pounds. You should therefore understand that in saying 'shop around', I am not saying that you should give up every solid business relationship that you've built up over the years merely to make a few small savings. This can prove to be quite expensive over the long term.

Having said that you should also avoid getting stuck in the rut of paying the same people the same high rates for the same mediocre service. Here are a few suggestions to help you 'shop around' more effectively:

- **Monitor rates and prices.** Keep your eyes and ears wide open to try to find out what people are paying their solicitors, mortgage brokers, insurers etc. You can do this by simply asking people and/or by paying close attention to advertisements on different media platforms. This will put you in a position to make solid decisions when considering a new provider, or perhaps to renegotiate what you pay your current provider.
- **Try to benefit from 'special rates' whenever you can.** It is sometimes the case that new service providers attempt to break into an existing market by offering significantly better deals than established players. You should carefully consider whether it would be beneficial to take them up on such offers (perhaps on a small scale at first until you have assessed their 'staying power'). Doing so could lead to a mutually beneficial long term relationship being established.
- **Attempt to obtain 'bulk discounts' where possible.** If you have built up a significant portfolio you can negotiate with service providers from a position of relative strength. Make the point that you can bring them a significant amount of business but that you expect lower rates/fees in return.

In light of the above, it would be a very good idea to go through your books on a regular basis and:

1) Evaluate what you are paying providers
2) Assess how valuable (in terms of service and delivery) your current providers are
3) Start shopping around in the cases where you feel you can do better!

# Not having a clear 'game plan'

At one stage it seemed that just about everybody and his dog was ready to enter the property market, simply because it was the 'done thing'! These days there are much fewer people rushing helter-skelter to get on the investment property ladder, but it still does not mean that everybody who is doing so, is doing it with a very clear idea of what they want to achieve through the property market.

Before taking the first steps toward investing in property, you should first sit down and clearly set out your reasons for wanting to do so. Doing this will not only help you develop a solid business plan later on, it will also enable you to be much more focused in your investment strategy since you know exactly where you want to be heading.

As a guide you should at the very least determine into which of the following categories you fall in terms of your own investment profile

- **Investors Seeking Regular Additional Income:** Investors in this category hope that property will eventually supplement their current income to a significant degree.
- **Investors Seeking Additional 'Lump Sum' Income:** These investors are not so much focused on regular income as they

are on boosting their assets through occasional large gains. This can be achieved either through buying and selling properties or through investing in property trusts.

- **Investors Pursuing Early Retirement:** Property can be a good way towards generating sufficient income to enable investors to take early retirement and to provide them with a steady income when they do.

- **Investors Seeking to Become Full Time Property Players:** People in this category see property as a career opportunity in which they would like to work towards 'quitting their day jobs' to become fully involved in property investment (as developers or landlords for example).

- **Investors Seeking to help their Children or Family:** It is a sad fact that it is extremely difficult for many people to 'get on the property ladder' these days. Many investors are therefore keen to take the opportunity to leverage their capital and experience in order to help their children to get a place of their own.

- **Investors Seeking Lifestyle Improvements:** Some investors design their strategy around eventually gaining a better property for themselves or to obtain a very desirable retirement property.

- **Investors Seeking to Raise Capital for other Investments:** Some people see property as a 'first step' towards bringing other investment goals (i.e. starting a business) to fruition. They are, therefore, largely focused on the realisation of fairly quick gains.

It should be clear from the above that there can be many different reasons for wanting to become involved in the property market. Before setting out you should determine into which of the above categories (if any!) you fall as this decision will ultimately affect the business and investment decisions that you will have to make as you get your business up and running.

# MISTAKE 48

# Not planning for the long-haul

It may seem like a world away but as recently as a few years ago people were still proclaiming the virtues of ultra short term strategies. Seminars were held to tell people to: Get In – Get Out – Make a Profit – Rinse and Repeat!

This obviously created an atmosphere which was seen as nothing more than the latest 'get rich quick 'scheme, where very quick profits could be made with a minimal level of effort and investment.

The creation of this mindset was bad news all round. For serious investors it meant having to compete with 'fly by night' operators who were only after a quick buck and were, therefore, giving the whole sector a bad name. For the general public it meant having to deal with a volatile property sector in which prices sometimes rose more due to speculative activities than due to market fundamentals. Needless to say, a lot of people got burned in the process!

It is it not all doom and gloom however. The current economic climate gives serious investors the opportunity to:

• Position themselves for the long-haul by consolidating and even expanding their portfolios. They can do this by making use of the good value that can currently be found in the market.

- Strengthen the fundamentals of their businesses by gaining long term tenants from those who left the market in a hurry.
- Gain a competitive advantage through having long term survival (and thriving!) strategies in place.

The most important point that I am trying to make is that you should do your best not to see property investment as simply a short term infatuation that you indulge while the market is 'hot', and then abandon at the first sign of trouble. Investors who do that cannot even be called proper investors but should rather be seen as speculators. In any speculative boom there are obviously some people who do well, especially in the initial stages. There are, however, many more who get burned, especially those who jump on the 'band wagon' towards the end.

You can avoid this kind of 'boom and bust' ride by positioning yourself for the long-haul. Make a commitment to yourself that you will build your business through both the good and the tough times and that you will use those tough times to your advantage. You will be amazed at the fantastic results that you can achieve over the long term.

What do General Electric, Disney, HP and Microsoft have in common? Answer: They were all started during times of serious economic downturn. If the big players on the world market understand the value of forward planning and 'staying the course' then we should all sit up, take notice, and follow their example!

# Not Determining your Risk Profile

All of us are different in the way in which we react to risk. Some people think nothing of hurling themselves off a bridge attached to a slender rope, while others see going to the other side of town as a major adventure. Our risk profiles are also reflected in the way in which we do business and how we work with money. It is, therefore, very important that you determine you own personal risk profile before becoming seriously involved in property investing. Doing so will help you to operate efficiently and in a way where you will not be constantly stressed out by facing risks that you feel incapable of handling.

The recent downturn in the housing market has actually been a very healthy corrective when it comes to investors' perceptions of the risks associated with the property market. For too long unscrupulous operators have been able to claim that it is 'risk free' and that all that you had to do was to plonk down your money to 'become a property millionaire in 12 months!' These days, people obviously find such claims much harder to stomach, which means that they are in a much better position to determine their own attitude towards risk.

As a general rule risk tends to be closely related to return on investment. Low Risk Investments more or less guarantee that you will get back at least what you originally put in, but the return on investment can sometimes be pitifully small. Higher Risk Investments hold out the possibility of much higher returns but obviously also of much bitter losses.

Determining your risk profile is simply a matter of evaluating how much money you have available to invest and how your life would be affected if the investment did not turn out as you hoped. In other words: How much of a 'hit' will I be able to take if necessary? It also has to do with your own psychological and emotional make up. If you are by nature very cautious, a very high risk investment strategy is almost guaranteed to give you sleepless nights.

As a general rule the following investments can be recommended at the different risk profile levels:

**Very Low Risk:** Cash or Deposit Accounts
**Low Risk:** Fixed Interest Accounts
**Medium Risk:** Managed Funds (i.e. investing in a property trust)
**Medium Risk to High Risk (Depending on the market):** Direct
**High Risk:** Direct Equity Investment in a single company (i.e. a property developer).

I want to make clear that the above does not mean that I am saying property is always a 'risky business'. Far from it! Property can still be seen as one of the safest forms of investment around. You should not, however, think that there will be no risk involved whatsoever, and a part of your strategy should be to clearly determine the level of risk with which you would be comfortable and then to tailor your investment strategy accordingly.

## MISTAKE 50

# Not investigating all the Options

Most new investors will think of just one thing when starting: buying residential properties in order to rent them out. While residential rentals are certainly a huge part of the investment property scene, it is by no means the whole game. You would, therefore, do well to also investigate some of the options open to you before committing yourself to a specific investment strategy. In general you should consider the following:

**Residential Property:** Residential property is certainly the easiest to get into and it does present some excellent opportunities for building up a thriving business. The downsides are that it can sometimes be extremely labour intensive and that returns on investment can sometimes be smaller than with other types of investment.

**Commercial Property:** Commercial Property (discussed in more detail elsewhere) can sometimes achieve excellent returns of investment as well as the benefits that come with a more stable tenant profile. The start up and management costs of a commercial property business can be significant however.

**Property Development:** Property Development is certainly not for the faint of heart, as the risks involved can be significant. It does, however, offer excellent returns on investment, as well as a very clearly defined business cycle. This is because activity in this sector is largely 'project based' which means that it is just the place to invest for people who like to move from project to project.

**Property Renovation:** Good profits can be made through buying run down properties, repairing them and placing them back on the market. This is a particularly attractive option for people with the necessary technical and/or project management skills. The main disadvantages are that it has become a rather crowded market due to the recent proliferation of television 'make over' shows. It also requires a very special skill set to keep building and restoration projects on schedule and on budget.

**Trusts:** Trusts offer investors the opportunities to enter market sectors that are normally closed to the smaller investor (e.g. large office block developments). It does this through pooling the resources of many investors in order to make investments in such projects. This has historically been seen as a very good investment, but recent returns have not been very good. The reason for this is that trusts are very exposed to the wider macroeconomic environment.

All of the above options clearly show that there are several excellent and potentially rewarding ways to become involved in the investment property market. The main things that you need to do are to

1) Determine where you want to start: It is quite likely that one of the options mentioned above will fit your skill-set and

circumstances much better than the others. That would obviously be the best place to start. You cannot, however, simply rest on your laurels once you have made that start. The second part of your strategy should therefore be to

2) Plan for diversification: The old saying about not putting all your eggs in one basket is, yet again, spot-on. You should therefore aim to diversify your portfolio and activities as early in your investment career as possible.

# Not planning for 'business threatening' events

No one sets out in business with the express purpose of closing down the business a few months or years down the line. However, it is a sad fact that personal, business or macro-economic developments often force business owners to reconsider their options. It is perhaps never pleasant to think about such things, but you would do yourself a huge favour if you could plan beforehand how you would react to certain circumstances and/or events.

Some of the things that you will need to consider are:

- **How will a possible marriage break-up affect my business?** Many small investors make use of tax strategies that utilise the allowances of both partners in a marriage. This can obviously have serious implications in case of divorce.
- **What will happen if I become sick or incapacitated?** Long term illness or injury (your own or that of a close family member) can have a serious negative impact on your ability to manage your business. Ask yourself how you will deal with this, should it occur?

- **How will losing my job affect my business?** Many investors rely heavily on regular salaried income during the early phases of their careers. Being made redundant can, therefore, directly impact their ability to continue running and expanding their businesses.

- **How will I deal with sudden demands for cash?** It is often the case that a major incident (e.g. structural damage to a property) can place enormous strain on a small investor's wallet. Therefore, you need to determine beforehand how you will deal with large, unforeseen, cash needs.

- **When will I decide to 'cut my losses'?** It is sadly sometimes the case that a business keeps losing money over an extended period. In such cases the response of business owners is often just to try and 'ride things out' while sustaining massive losses along the way, and then having to close down the business anyway. As a business owner you will have to 'draw a line in the sand' beforehand as far as losses go. Doing this before you even start your business will help you to put your exit plan in action should the need for it actually arise.

- **What will happen to my business when I die?** Proper estate planning should be an integral part of every person's life. So much more so in the case of the small business owner. Your death will not only affect your loved ones (who could be left with serious liabilities if you do not plan well) but also tenants and business partners. You should, therefore, plan your will very carefully and leave clear instructions on what should happen with every single part of your business at the time of your death.

# Not having back-up strategies in place

The previous section referred to planning your response in the face of certain 'business threatening' events. One very important part of this planning should be to have solid strategies in place to deal with some of these events. Some of the things that you should seriously consider doing are the following:

**Cover yourself against possible loss of income during times of illness:** There are some very good insurance policies available that can protect your income during times of serious illness. Speak to a financial advisor about setting up such a policy. You will certainly sleep a little bit better at night if you do!

**Cover yourself against the financial implications of losing your job:** Many insurance companies will, at a premium of course, insure you against the possible loss of your main source of income. You can normally choose different levels of cover and for how long you would like benefits to be paid.

**Clarify your legal position:** It is very important that you have a solid understanding of what your position would be in the case of a marriage break-up. A solicitor should be able to help you and your partner to assess this and also to draw up contracts in such a way that that it gives you and your spouse the maximum tax benefits as well as the best possible individual protection. This is obviously quite a complicated area and you would be well advised to appoint a solicitor with a great deal of experience in these kinds of matters.

**Set up a contingency fund:** The best way to deal with sudden demands for large amounts of cash would be to have funds available that were set aside specifically for this purpose. The setting up and management of contingency funds are discussed in more detail elsewhere in the book, but allow me to emphasise their immense importance to the long term survival of your business.

**Have a clear 'exit strategy':** Drawing a 'line in the sand' in terms of how much loss you are willing to sustain is not enough. You will also have to set out very clearly what you will do should you ever reach that line. Planning for this and putting it in writing could help you a great deal should this ever happen.

**Get your will in order:** Make very sure that your will goes way beyond your personal effects and circumstances. You should ideally also have some kind of 'business will' in place. A solicitor can help you to attach or combine this with your general will. Such a document should spell out in great detail what should happen with different parts of your business. Having this in place can save your family from a great deal of head scratching and even from serious hardship.

None of us would obviously like to see any of the events described above happening to us. But to pretend that such events do not happen, or that if they do, they will not have a serious impact on your business, is to be like an ostrich with its head in the sand!

# MISTAKE 53

# Not investigating
# different scenarios

There is an old saying that the only constant in life is change. You would do well to remember this throughout your investment career! You may plan to enter business under certain

1) Economic Conditions
2) Personal Circumstances
3) Social Conditions and
4) Demographic Realities.

There are no guarantees that these will stay the same, however. In fact, if you remain in business for some time it is quite likely that each of these factors will change several times over the course of the years. Therefore, you should do your best to engage in a bit of 'futurology' to try to determine how your business is likely to cope under changed circumstances.

Trying to determine future trends does not entail getting out the old crystal ball or dabbling in the 'dark arts'! It can simply be a matter of trying to determine the answers to some very basic questions. These are:

1) **How will increased costs affect my 'bottom line'?** Try to get a very good idea of what your costs would be and then

'crunch the numbers' to see what a 10%, 20% and 30% increase would do to your business. How much of this percentage do you think that you would be able to decrease through better cost management? How much would you be able to absorb? Where is the 'point of no return'? Are you perhaps too close to it already?

2) **What changes do you see happening in your target market, and will it affect you should it continue?** It may be that you are already seeing some changes happening in the area where you are investing, or planning to invest. Perhaps there is a bit of gentrification going on, or perhaps more young people are moving in. What would the likely impact be should you extrapolate these changes over the next decades? (It may be that the area turning into 'yuppie heaven' could spell bad news for your 'bargain basement' portfolio and that you will have to adapt or die!)

3) **What is the macro-economic trend and how will it affect the property market?** This is perhaps a difficult question to answer in detail if you are not an academic economist. We can however, on a slightly less technical level, all try to determine the way the 'wind is blowing' by keeping pace with the news, listening closely to conversations, and monitoring the activity in our businesses. Using all of these to develop a sense of where the economy is heading can be an invaluable business tool.

4) **Are there specific changes in the economy of the local area that I will have to consider?** Make sure that you keep close tabs on the area in which you are investing. Keeping your finger on the pulse could enable you to be first in line to offer accommodation to students at a new campus, or to get out of the market in time before the closure of a major factory.

# Missing out on opportunities to buy new-build properties

During the height of the housing boom thousands of people were buying and selling properties 'off plan' without ever setting foot in them. In some cases properties were even bought and sold several times before they were actually completed. Those days are obviously long gone as the pace of investment driven development has slowed dramatically. This does not mean, however, that there are not still fantastic opportunities available when it comes to the buying and selling of newly developed properties.

The main benefits to buying 'off plan' are:

- You can potentially get a very good return on investment, especially if the property is in a highly desirable development or general area.

- A strategic benefit to buying "off-plan" and selling is that your initial costs can be quite a bit lower than with other investments, as you are only planning to hang on to the property long enough for it to sell. Therefore, you only have to raise the deposit and enough money to cover payments until completion. This obviously means that this is an investment much better suited to markets in which properties are selling rapidly.

- It is not a very labour intensive way of investing, as you don't have to spend a lot of time to manage or renovate properties.

It should be clear from this that buying in new developments can sometimes yield some very positive outcomes. You should, however, make sure that you do your homework very thoroughly before you commit yourself, especially in the current market. This is because there are also some very real risk factors associated with buying 'off plan'.

- New build developments are often marketed aggressively with a lot of hype about investment opportunities thrown into the mix. It is therefore not always very easy to separate the fact from the fluff and secure a truly excellent investment.
- New properties are typically sold at much higher rates than existing ones. This means that the prices have to rise quite quickly and by quite a margin for you to make a profit. This obviously increases the importance of sourcing the right property in the right area.
- It can sometimes be risky to put pen to paper on a property that will only be completed in a few month's time. Market conditions can obviously change dramatically during that time, perhaps leaving you with a property that is difficult to offload.

All of the above means that you will have to do a great deal of solid research before deciding to enter this potentially lucrative, but also volatile, market. You should also realise that buying 'off plan' is a relatively high risk strategy. This means that you will need to understand your own risk profile and then determine whether you are willing to take the plunge!

# Buying 'off plan' without doing your homework

There is often so much hype and razzle-dazzle involved in the marketing of new-build properties that it is difficult to make a rational decision on buying one for investment purposes, or if you do decide to buy one, where and what kind of property to purchase. You can deal with this problem by following a clearly defined strategy, should you decide to go down this route. The central plank of this strategy should be **research**! Use this to make sure that you get the best possible property, at the best possible location, and at the best possible price.

It goes without saying that 'research' does not simply mean studying the marketing claims of all the different developments! You should instead take on the role of a true property 'Sherlock Holmes' in order to sniff out the best opportunities. Some of the ways in which you can maximise your chances of doing this are:

• **Try to find properties that are in the very early stages of development:** Developers need a lot of cash to get a building project off the ground. Having some investors on board from the word go can help with this. It can also add some credibility to a new and relatively unknown project. Because of this developers will sometimes be willing to offer substantial discounts to the first few buyers. Do your best to be one of them!

- **Study the plans carefully:** Developers always have properties that they want to shift first and will therefore market them heavily to anyone who enquires. The problem is that these are often the units that they know they will struggle to sell later on (due to the lack of a good view, lack of sunlight, proximity to a road etc.) when the project has moved from planning to conception. Do not be hoodwinked by this! Make sure that you study all plans carefully and take them to a professional architect if you have difficulty in interpreting them properly. Always be on the lookout for unique features that are likely to increase the desirability of the property.

- **Visit the site:** It is amazing to see how many people buy properties in places where they have never even set foot. This could have worked during the boom times but it is akin to economic suicide under the current circumstances. If you do plan to buy within a new development you should pay a few visits to the site beforehand. This should give you a good understanding of the location (Is it in the middle of nowhere or will it attract people due to its proximity to amenities?), infrastructure (Is everything in place to service the area? Look at the quality of the roads, communications infrastructure and services), and the local area (Is the local area ready for the development? Will it fit in? Is there a need for all the extra dwellings?)

Doing your homework and asking and answering all the right questions can mean the difference between getting a great asset, or saddling yourself with a liability. You should, therefore, make sure that you take all the necessary steps of due diligence before entering into any negotiations about a property in a new development.

# Not negotiating the best price when buying 'off plan'

When buying off plan your primary objective is usually to sell the property at a profit as soon as possible. It does not take a rocket scientist to work out that you can maximise your chances of doing this by limiting the amount that you pay for the property as much as you can. The good news is that it is often possible to negotiate a substantial discount on the initial asking price if you play your cards right. Some strategies that you should keep in mind are the following:

- **Try to get on board from the beginning:** Developers will often offer the first few buyers substantial discounts as their 'buying in' translates into an increased cash flow for the project. Having early buyers also strengthens the project's credibility and the fact that some people already have put pen to paper is often used in marketing new developments.

- **Try to buy one of the last available units:** This strategy is the exact opposite of the one mentioned above. Developers are often desperate to 'sign off' on a site towards the end of a project, as this will enable them to focus all their attention on new projects. They may be quite willing to negotiate if you make it clear that you are interested in helping them move on!

- **Try to negotiate as close to the end of the developer's financial year as possible:** This strategy obviously takes some planning and research but this could very well be worth your while. Most big developers have very ambitious sales targets and their executives know that shareholders and clients react favourably to these being reached. A lower offer is, therefore, much more likely to be accepted during a time when these targets are being chased aggressively.

- **Try to get a 'volume discount':** If you are in a position to buy more than one property in a development it can obviously strengthen your hand immensely. You should therefore always make your willingness to purchase two or more properties at a reduced price clear to the developer.

- **Try to obtain as many 'value added' benefits as possible:** It may sometimes be the case that developers are unable to offer discounts but are willing to add some other value to a property (e.g. by finishing it to a higher standard or by adding 'top of the range' appliances). This can in some cases be as good as a cash discount, since it could make a real difference to the price that you can eventually set for the property. Just make sure that you are not hoodwinked into accepting the same 'special features' that everybody else is getting!

The main notion that you need to keep in mind when negotiating a discount is that it should be a real discount! Developers often artificially inflate prices on properties and then they offer a 'discount' on this! Make sure that you do not fall for this trick but that you do everything within your power to get as much 'bang for your buck' as possible!

# Shying away from renovation projects

Property renovation has a pretty bad image these days. We are constantly regaled by property shows with 'tales of woe' showing us how badly people got burned in trying to bring a 'fixer upper' to the market. The main reasons for this are usually **a)** Massive cost overruns as people totally under-estimate how much money they will have to put down to get a place presentable again and **b)** Massive frustration as projects just keep dragging on with no end in sight.

I have no illusions about the fact the above just about sums up the experience of most people in trying to renovate properties. However, to think that this is everything that there is to say is to grossly under-estimate the potential for excellent returns on investment that can still be found in this area. The benefits of renovation (done in the right way of course) can be summarised as follows:

- **Quick turn-around times:** If you manage projects well (and that is indeed a big if!) you can turn a profit or have a fabulous place ready for tenants in a matter of months.

- **Solid returns on investment:** Contrary to what the property shows will have you believe, there are still some properties out there that can be bought cheaply and then renovated at relatively minor cost. Some very good profits can still be made this way. The trick is of course to find these properties before anyone else does!

- **Incentives and tax-breaks:** It is often possible to access preservation grants and tax breaks (such as savings on VAT) while you are working on older properties. It could also be that grants may be available to help you make a property more energy efficient. All of this can, of course, make a huge difference to what you will have to spend to get a property ready for the market or tenants.

- **Customisation:** Renovating a property sometimes means that you are working with a 'blank slate' in terms of what the final product will look like. The main benefit of this is that you can target the end product directly at your ideal tenants or your potential buyers. This can have a very positive effect on your ability to let or sell the property eventually.

Renovation is obviously not for everyone. You will need lots of time and patience to pull it off. You will also need a skill-set that is particularly strong on working with your hands and/or project management. If you have all of this and you do decide to go down this route, you may very well find that it is one of the best decisions you have ever made!

# Rushing blindly into renovation projects

In the previous section we had a look at all the good reasons why you should perhaps consider becoming involved in renovation projects. This section deals with the other side of the coin, namely why some people should perhaps stay away as far as possible from them. Please note that I am not contradicting myself here. Property renovation can certainly be a good idea for some **if** they have the right psychological make-up and skill set. Other people should perhaps rather consider other options. The main reasons behind this advice are:

- **Relatively large financial outlay:** If you buy a relatively intact property your main costs will be the deposit and legal costs. With a renovation property it will be all of the above plus a substantial amount of money to spend on the renovation. This can lead to cash flow problems and a relatively longer time before the initial investment is recovered.
- **Competition:** There is often stiff competition for 'fixer-uppers'. This obviously drives the prices up, minimising the benefits that could have been gained from buying the property at a lower price and then bringing it to the market.

- **Market Volatility:** In economically uncertain times the actual time that it takes to fix the property can mean that the market has changed a great deal from the time when the property was purchased to when it re-enters the market to be sold or let.
- **Uncertainty:** You are never certain what you will find under the floorboard or in the roof. You could, for example, be asked to pay for the costly process of removing traces of asbestos from the property.
- **Bureaucracy:** You will have to get planning permission and/or buldings regulations consent for major changes. These processes that could keep you, your architect, or your solicitor so busy that the initial benefit of buying a cheaper property gets lost.
- **Legal and Statutory requirements:** You will have to comply with all relevant workplace regulations (including 'Health and Safety Law) while the project is being undertaken. The costs related to this (especially indemnity insurance) can be significant.

Added to all of this there are the factors that we have already mentioned, namely that projects often take longer and cost more than was initially thought. You can protect yourself against all of this by making sure that you have the capacity and skill-set to undertake the project, and by then handling it as a professional project to be completed as quickly and as efficiently as possible. The greatest pitfall that you will have to avoid in this regard is to treat the project as a little 'hobby project'. Doing this will slow things down and will cause some people to lose respect for what you are doing. You should also remember that even though 'doing a place up' might sound like a bit of fun, you are not paying for the improvements with Monopoly money!

# Not taking out adequate insurance when renovating

The importance of being properly insured as a landlord has already been discussed in a previous chapter. What many landlords don't realise, however, is that this general principle is just as applicable, if not more so, during times when they are renovating a property in order to get it ready for the market.

Some of the areas/events for which you will have to consider insurance cover are:

**Public Liability Cover:** This is especially important if the property is going to remain empty for an extended period.

**Insurance to cover the work that is being undertaken:** Your building project is costing you money and adding value to the property. It does not make sense, therefore, just to cover the outcome at the end. You should also cover the work as it takes place. This means that you will be covered for the loss of time and value if the effects of your renovation are damaged by a flood or fire before the project is complete. This kind of insurance will also often cover you against structural damage to a building as a result of your project.

**Legal Expenses Cover:** None of us set out wanting to go to court but this possibility may arise during your project (e.g. if you have a very serious dispute with one of the contractors). Having proper cover in place can put you in a much stronger position to stand your ground.

**Employers Liability Cover:** This is absolutely essential if you are managing the project yourself and employing people to help you. If you are making use of an independent contractor you should make sure that they hold adequate insurance.

**On-site materials and equipment:** It is likely that there will be thousands of pounds worth of equipment at your property for extended periods. Ensure that it is covered against theft and accidental damage.

**Contents Insurance:** If you are going to live in the property during the time when the renovation takes place, you are obviously going to need insurance for your personal belongings and effects. This can sometimes be included in a 'broader' insurance policy.

**Personal Accident and Disability Cover:** Have you ever considered what will happen to the project, and your income, if you cannot pay attention to it for a few months? This type of cover provides income protection in the case of this eventuality.

If all of this makes your head spin, take heart! It is not necessary to put together a package containing all the elements mentioned above yourself. A specialist property insurance broker can help you to determine your exact needs and can then tailor-make a package designed to address them. Doing it this way will often be much cheaper than trying to cobble together your own insurance solution.

Whatever you do, make sure that you protect yourself against the nasty surprises that can sometimes come with property renovation – you probably have enough other things to worry about already!

## MISTAKE 60

# Not refurbishing and furnishing according to market needs (1)

One of the first things that a would-be landlord should do is to move away from the idea that all properties and tenants have been created equal and that they could, therefore, just create some kind of 'generic template' that tenants will adapt to. If you do this, you are missing out on some of the very real benefits that come with specialisation and a market focused approach. You should take great care to research your target market and then make sure that your properties meet their criteria as closely as possible.

There are different market segments on which you could focus, but for the sake of brevity this chapter will highlight the five that you are most likely to encounter. They are: Students, Professionals, Families, Social Tenants and Independent older people.

Let us look at the needs of each of the above market segments in turn:

**Students:** The student market can be very tough and competitive. It is also more labour intensive than the other types. Make sure that you have the edge over your competition by offering properties with the following features:

- Properties that are easy to clean and maintain both inside and outside
- A large common area with comfortable furniture
- A kitchen with ample storage space and room for a large fridge-freezer combination
- Separate toilets
- More than one bathroom
- A wireless network offering flat rate access to the internet will certainly score very highly on prospective tenants' wish lists

**Young Professionals:** Young professionals often band together to rent a house or a flat with the expectation that every person will have his/her own room. It is quite a lucrative market to enter into and it also tends to be less labour intensive than catering for students. Some of the things that you should try to offer are:

- High quality and 'trendy' finishes.
- Hi-tech appliances
- Properties that are easy to maintain and clean
- Dedicated parking areas
- Lots of built-in storage space, both in the kitchen and in the bedrooms
- An outside area that could possibly be used for entertaining
- The more en-suite rooms you have available the better you will do in this market segment
- As with the student market the provision of a wireless network will certainly boost your ratings!

Obviously, not every single property in your portfolio will be able to tick all of these boxes. The main thing that you need to keep in mind, however, is that these are the kinds of things that are considered important by these groups. You should also not stop at this simple list; conducting a bit of market research will help you to pitch your properties exactly right for those to whom you are marketing it.

The next chapter will focus on targeting your properties towards families, older individuals and social tenants.

# Not renovating and furnishing according to market needs (2)

This chapter follows on from the previous one in discussing some of the things that you need to keep in mind when preparing your property, and then marketing it to different market segments. This is of vital importance if you want to achieve the highest possible occupation rates and rental returns. The focus in this chapter will be on families, older individuals and social tenants.

**Families:** With families, the focus should obviously be on creating a home that can function effectively as the hub of a family. Some of the things that parents will look out for are:

- Good durable finishes with a light and airy feel
- Safety features, especially if they have very young children
- A kitchen and/or dining area that is large enough to easily accommodate the whole family
- Floors that are easy to clean
- More than one bathroom with one being en-suite
- Ample outside space with an easy to maintain garden
- Dedicated parking space, if possible for more than one vehicle

**Older Individuals:** Older professionals who are ready to 'scale down', perhaps after the kids have left home, are a growing presence in the rental property market. They tend to want smaller, easy to maintain properties that are close to transport links. Some of the other things that you could perhaps do to make the property appealing to them are the following:

- If the property has any period features it might be a good idea to enhance and highlight them.
- Try to stay away from super trendy designs and finishes, and make sure that all appliances and equipments are easy to use.
- A well appointed guest room is a big plus with this group, as these tenants want to have space available should the family and grandchildren come for a visit.

**Social Tenants:** The whole issue of renting to social tenants has been discussed in a previous chapter. Suffice it to say here that they are perhaps one of the easiest groups to prepare for, as the local council will very often supply you with a list of features, fixtures and fittings that you should install at the property before a long term rental can commence. This obviously removes a lot of the guesswork that is often part of preparing a property for occupation.

All of the above may sound like unnecessary expense and hassle, but I can assure you that if you look after the market then the market will look after you! This does not mean that you have to go over the top and blow your whole budget to create a piece of paradise. It just means that it cannot hurt to be seen as a responsive landlord who knows his market and how to best serve that market. This will set you apart from the masses of people who have a simple 'if you build it they will come' approach and who are constantly scratching their head over why they cannot attract and retain top quality tenants.

## MISTAKE 62

# Missing out on opportunities offered by auctions

Most people immediately see some red lights flashing when hearing the word 'auction'. However, as a property investor you should not automatically have this response, as there can sometimes be very significant benefits to buying properties at auction. Some of these include:

**Certainty and Control:** Negotiating sale prices can be a time-consuming, costly and prolonged process. The worst thing is that you are not certain of the outcome until the final exchange takes place. Auctions can eliminate this stress and uncertainty. You can take full control of what you are willing to pay for a property and then bid accordingly. If your bid is accepted it is final; the seller cannot later change his/her mind and easily walk away from the sale. If you are, therefore, in need of a property in a hurry, and you know exactly what you want to pay, then an auction may be the best route to go.

**Speed:** Buying at auction can also help you to avoid the drawn-out legal and bureaucratic processes that are part and parcel of normal property sales. Settlement after auction sales takes place much quicker, and you can take ownership of a property bought at auction in a matter of days after the event.

**Diversification:** Plugging in to one of the networks through which auctions are advertised can be an extremely effective way to diversify your property portfolio, as it will almost certainly bring to your attention properties that you would never otherwise have considered.

**Price:** Properties are sold at auction for a variety of reasons, but it often has to do with the seller (or a financial institution) wanting to achieve a very quick sale. It could also be that sellers are desperate to get rid of a property after failing to sell it on the open market. This all means that it is often possible to buy properties at auction at prices that are well below prices on the open market.

Buying at auction is obviously not everyone's cup of tea. You should, however, at least consider the possibility of whether it could not perhaps be one of the ways in which you can expand your portfolio. One way to start this investigation is to familiarise yourself with the auction process by attending a few auctions for properties that you have no intention of buying. This will help you to determine whether auctions should be part of your mode of operation and, if so, what the best strategies to follow would be. Doing this could quite possibly introduce you to a new world of opportunity that might allow you to grow your business much faster than would otherwise have been possible.

# MISTAKE 63

# Not being aware of some of the pitfalls of buying at auction

The previous chapter focused on some of the very real benefits that can be gained through buying a property at auction. There is, however, also another side to this story. Many inexperienced investors do not realise that agents and sellers will often do their best to manipulate the auction process to their advantage. It is, therefore, very important to make sure that you are familiar with the process, and with what to look out for, before you even place your first bid. Some of the things that require careful consideration are:

'Under quoting': It is common for sellers and their agents to quote a very low (and unrealistic) price as the likely selling price at an auction. They do this in the hope that more people will turn up and that the presence of so many potential bidders will translate into a bidding war. Unfortunately, this means that potential buyers often waste time by doing all the necessary preparation for the auction (e.g. arranging finance and even having surveys done) only to see the property sell for an amount way above what they were planning to offer. This practice is obviously quite unethical as it wastes the potential buyers' time and money, but there does not seem to be any indication of it being stamped out. The best way to avoid falling into this trap is to remember the old rule: If something is too good to be true, it probably is too good to be true!

**Getting 'carried away'**: The competitive atmosphere at auctions sometimes 'gets' to some people, causing them to place bids that are way over the odds simply because they relish the opportunity of 'beating' the other bidders. You can decide for yourself if it really is a 'victory' to pay too much for a property! If you suspect that you might have a problem in this area it would be better to appoint an agent to bid on your behalf.

**'Dummy Bidding'**: Some auctioneers use slightly dodgy tactics to move the bidding along at auctions. Most common among these is the practice of 'dummy bidding' where the auctioneer appoints a friend or colleague to place false bids simply to keep the excitement of the chase going and to so achieve a higher price (or to at least reach the reserve price). There are various official moves afoot to stop this practice but it will most likely continue as long as auctions take place. You can protect yourself by setting your absolute maximum bid beforehand and then sticking to it under all circumstances.

If all of the above makes you feel slightly nervous, don't worry! Auctions can still be one of the best ways to acquire value for money property. You just need to make sure that you approach them in a studied and professional way. Doing this will protect you from being hoodwinked into attending, bidding on the basis of emotions, or being fooled by an auctioneer's attempts to move the bidding along. We will focus on how this can actually be achieved in the next chapter.

## MISTAKE 64

# Not having a proper strategy in place when attempting to buy at auction

Like so many things in life, buying at auction is done best when it is done on the basis of a proper and well thought out strategy. The purpose of this chapter is to sketch the possible outlines of such a strategy. Following these simple steps will help to move you from an 'also ran' to someone who regularly hears the sweet sound of the gavel as it rewards you with another great deal!

- **Make sure that you understand the auction process in general and the rules of the specific auction in particular:** Investing time in understanding the culture, rules and outcomes of auctions will be time well spent as it will make you much less likely to make some very expensive blunders. I would, therefore, recommend that you become a 'student of auctions' for a few weeks before placing your very first bid. In doing so, you will quickly realise that success at auctions is not normally due to blind luck, but that it has a lot to do with solid preparation.

- **Carefully investigate the area of the property to be auctioned:** One of the best ways to ensure that you do not bid too much at an auction is to be sure of how much a property is actually worth! Having this information will also protect you from missing out on the 'deal of the decade'. All of this means that you should diligently research the local area before turning up for the auction. Of particular interest to you should be the average selling prices for similar properties compared to the one that is being auctioned. You can get this information by paying careful attention to the local media or through buying a formal report on the area.

- **Be Prepared:** If you are certain that you want to enter the bidding for a particular property as a serious player you should ensure that you arrive at the auction as well prepared as possible. This means, amongst other things, that you should have ascertained that there are no legal, technical or any other issues with the property. You should also be aware of any deficiencies and of how it is likely to affect the final price. Access to the necessary funds to pay the deposit is also essential. This means that you will have to inform your financial institution that you intend to bid at an auction, and get their approval. This will help to avoid some potentially embarrassing surprises later on.

- **Draw up a 'bidding plan' and stick to it:** You should plan, before you enter the room where the auction will be held, when you will enter the bidding and at what stage you will leave it (if necessary). Having such a plan in place will keep you from bidding in an irrational and over-excited manner. It may help to write these figures on a piece of paper as a reminder.

# Not viewing properties according to a predetermined plan

It is amazing and sad to see just how little time some potential landlords spend in actually viewing and surveying properties that they are looking to buy. This is all the more shocking when you stop to consider the fact that buying a particular property is likely to be one of the biggest transactions that they will ever enter into. It makes almost no business sense to spend so little time in selecting the very thing that will form the cornerstone of your property business, namely the property itself!

You can avoid this pitfall by arranging at least two viewings of every property that you are interested in buying. The first one can simply be your standard 'walk through' viewing where you get a general sense and feel of the property. You can then use this as the basis upon which to decide whether you will request a second. The second viewing is where the real work starts as you should use it to carefully determine whether the property will be the right 'fit' for your portfolio. Some of the things that you should do at this viewing include the following:

- **Make a simple line drawing of the layout of the property:** This will help you to carefully think over the potential of the property when you get home. It can also show you what possible changes will have to be made for the property to fulfil its intended purpose.

- **Note the general condition, as well as defects and issues that will need to be addressed:** Make a list of things that you think may need attention in the future. This will assist you in making the final decision as it will highlight the possible cost implications of likely alterations, corrections and modifications.

- **Take as many measurements as possible:** This will, again, help you to decide whether the property is fit for purpose. Having accurate measurements can also be of great assistance should you want to get formal quotations for any possible alterations.

- **Investigate the state of common areas (if any):** If the property is situated in a generally run down, badly managed development it will almost certainly affect the rent you can charge and the quality of tenants that you will attract. You should, therefore, spend some time to determine whether the development, and the wider area, is somewhere where people would want to live.

- **Take professionals with you if necessary:** If you know that the property is going to require a great deal of alteration it would be a very good idea to take some tradespersons with you to the viewing. They should be able to give you lots of advice on the state of the property, what is possible in terms of alterations, and what it is likely to cost.

- **Make notes on the structure of the property:** If you plan to do major alterations you should, at the viewing, determine which walls are load-bearing as this will obviously have direct implications for what you can change and where.

Doing all of the above may seem like a lot of work. It is nothing, however, if you compare it to the amount of work that you are going to have to do to manage or dispose of a property that is not a perfect fit for your portfolio.

# Unrealistic pricing and hanging on too long when trying to sell a property

There comes a time in the career of every investor when it becomes necessary to dispose of one or more properties. This is perhaps one of the most challenging things to do well, especially as most investors struggle not to be too emotionally involved in the process.

The best way to minimise the stress often associated with selling properties is to get as much good advice as possible about pricing the property before you put it on the market. This will help you to set the price at a level where you will attract as many potential buyers as possible at the best price possible. Achieving this is obviously no mean feat and getting it right requires a great deal of study, patience and good advice! It also requires a solid dose of realism about what is achievable under current market conditions. During boom times, when it seems like the only way is up, this is obviously not much of a concern, since there will always be eager buyers to help correct your mistake. During more difficult times setting a realistic price is a vital skill.

As with so many other things, keeping your ear to the ground, doing solid research and doing a bit of due diligence are all key when attempting to set a realistic price. Do your best to try to find out what properties similar to yours sold for and what strategies were followed to achieve those prices. The final price that you decide on may be a big disappointment when you compare it to what you could perhaps have achieved for the property in the past. It is no use crying over spilt milk, however; your task is so achieve a realistic price under current circumstances, not those of a few years back!

When you have set your price you should take great care to let the property go at just the right moment. There is a fine balance to be struck between holding out for a better price and doing the best under the current circumstances. One thing to consider is that it very rarely costs you nothing to hold on to a property! The mortgage, insurance, possible council tax, etc. will still have to be paid. You should, therefore, very carefully crunch the numbers to determine when holding on will actually start to cost you more than what you are likely to gain by letting go.

# Not investigating all the options, including holiday letting

We all have different dreams and needs when it comes to holidays, but those who often spend extended periods in the same UK area every year would do well to investigate the possibility of acquiring a holiday home to let out. This property can then be used for your own holidays as well as the generation of income (holiday homes attract much higher weekly rentals). This option is certainly not for everyone and you will have to do your sums very carefully to determine whether it will be worth your while.

The first thing that you will need to realise is that there are certain special conditions that will have to be met if you want to claim business expenses and tax relief on a holiday let. These include:

- The property must be in the United Kingdom
- It has to be available to holidaymakers for at least 140 days a year (Note: This does not mean that you should be able to prove that you had tenants for this whole period. Using advertisements and other marketing material to show that it was available should be sufficient proof)

- You should be able to prove that you had paying guests in the property for at least half of the 140 days mentioned above.
- The property cannot be let to the same person for more than 31 days over a seven month period.

The first step in deciding to go down this route would obviously be to 'crunch the numbers' to try to determine how much income you are likely to generate from the property. An important factor to include in your calculations is whether you will be using the property for your own holidays as well. If this is the case you should include the potential savings in the sums.

How much you will be able to charge will obviously depend on several factors. These include:

- The length of the holiday season: Does the town or resort attract all year visitors or does it experience a relatively short 'high-season'? If all your income will be dependent on the latter, you will perhaps struggle to balance the books at the end of the year.
- Location: Is the property in which you are interested located in a recognised tourist area? It is all well and good to try to break new ground by getting tourists to come to a new area, but it is also a strategy than can backfire spectacularly. It might, therefore, be better to leave promotional activity to the local tourist office!
- Suitability: Not every property can function effectively as a holiday let, and in many places all of those that can have more or less been snapped up. You should, therefore, do your homework to see whether properties are available and, if so, whether they can be used for this purpose. (Some local councils will prevent investors from starting new holiday homes in areas that they believe are already saturated)

MISTAKE **68**

# Not managing a holiday let professionally

Many people make the mistake of deciding to invest in a holiday home based on little more than a whim. This often happens while they are on holiday at a certain resort and they start to toy with the idea of owning a property there. This is obviously no way to run a business! If you do decide to invest in a holiday property you should do it with a proper understanding of everything that will be required to make it a success. Here are some of the things that you will have to keep in mind:

**Invest enough time and money in furnishing and renovating the property:** One of the reasons that people go on holiday is to escape from the daily grind: they prefer their holiday accommodation not to be 'more of the same'. You should, therefore, try and take some extra trouble to furnish and decorate the property to a high standard. Anything that could enhance the holiday experience (i.e. a Jacuzzi) will also help you to achieve a better return on investment. All of this may seem like unnecessary expense, but I can assure you that it will be money well spent.

**Put good management and communication systems in place:** You will have to deal with multiple tenants on a weekly basis during the holiday season. This can obviously add significantly to your workload, and you should, therefore, work on ways to streamline the whole process of managing, letting and marketing the property. One solution could be to market the property on the internet through a website that provides facilities for online bookings.

**Try to minimise costs:** Letting expenses (e.g. insurance) are often quite a bit higher for holiday lets than for 'normal' properties. Do your best to minimise these costs through shopping around for the best deals.

**Appoint a reliable agent if necessary:** It is quite likely that you will live some distance away from the property, which means that it might be difficult to visit regularly. This may make it necessary to appoint an agent to manage the property on your behalf. All of the normal principles for selecting agents will apply in such a case. You should also take extra care to appoint an agent with knowledge of, and experience in, the holiday letting market.

**Try to limit the effects of seasonality:** One of the most frustrating things about managing a holiday let is the fact that many resorts operate according to very clearly defined seasons. This means that you will sometimes have too many enquiries to handle, only to face extended 'dry periods' just a few weeks later. You should try to minimise this effect by selecting a property in a resort where the season is relatively long or, even better, a resort which attracts visitors throughout the year. Your marketing efforts should also focus on attracting customers outside the traditional peak seasons.

## MISTAKE 69

# Not marketing a holiday let effectively

The number one reason why people eventually get rid of holiday lets is the fact that they feel that it is a constant struggle to get enough people through to balance the books. This is obviously no mean feat, since you will have to generate new prospects just about every week during the season (and beyond). It is, therefore, extremely important that you have a solid and workable marketing plan in place before you enter the holiday letting market. Some of the basic principles that you will have to keep in mind are:

- **Your marketing needs to be constant:** Do your best to avoid cycles of 'famine and feast'. You can do this by keeping up a constant marketing campaign. You will, therefore, have to keep up your marketing efforts even during times when you have enough customers.
- **Your marketing needs to be targeted:** Do your best to reach people who are actually 'in the market' for the kind of holiday experience that you can offer. This means that you will perhaps have to find creative ways to reach new audiences.

- **Good service is one of the most important parts of marketing:** It has been shown time and time again that 'word of mouth' is one of the top factors upon which people base their holiday decisions. The flashiest marketing campaign will mean nothing if it is not supported by excellent levels of service once people respond to it.

  Here are some specific ways in which you can market your property:

- **Use your guests:** This ties in with the last point above. Satisfied customers can be your most effective sales tool. Make sure that you have plenty of marketing materials on hand that they can take home with them (e.g. brochures) or that they can send to their friends (e.g. postcards). Also ask their permission to contact them in the future with news about your property.

- **Make use of special offers:** Finding customers for the "off season" can make a real difference to your business, as it will bring in more cash than you require for running expenses. Offering the property at reduced rates or through 'pay for one week, get another one free' should therefore form an integral part of your marketing efforts.

- **Find the best marketing outlets possible:** Do some research about your target customers and especially about the media that they consume. This will in the end provide you with a list of publications that you can use for a highly targeted marketing campaign.

- **Make use of the internet:** More and more people are going online to find the best holiday experiences. You should, therefore, make sure that you are online too! A simple website will cost very little to set up but can be invaluable in generating leads. You should also consider registering with one of the many websites that offer online marketing and booking services.

# Not doing your homework
# when buying a tenanted property

It is sometimes advisable for new investors to buy a property with tenants already in place. In this kind of situation you essentially 'take over' the tenants from the previous landlord. This may seem like a very neat and painless solution to the problem of acquiring your first tenants. It can also be a bit easier to get finance on a tenanted property as the fact that it has already been let demonstrates earning potential. You will however have to go through the necessary steps of due diligence in order to ensure that you are not just taking over someone else's difficulties. There are, therefore, some very important questions that you will have to ask before proceeding with the transaction. These include the following:

**Are the tenants reliable?** This should be your starting point in determining whether you should 'take them over'. Do your best to find out whether the tenants have looked after the property and have paid their rent on time. If this is not the case you would obviously want to think twice about allowing them into your life.

**Why is the landlord selling?** Knowing the landlord's reason for selling the property can also help you in the final decision. Could it be that he is having problems with the tenants, or that the property is costing too much to maintain? Or that the neighbours are causing trouble in some way? If there are problems the landlord would obviously be quite reluctant to confide in you. You should therefore think of creative ways in which you can make your enquiries.

**Are the tenants really planning to stay on?** Many a landlord has found that 'sitting tenants' are often nothing of the sort! Make very sure that the tenants in the property are indeed eager to stay on in the property and that they would be willing to enter into a new agreement with you.

**How much is it costing to run the property?** One of the advantages of buying a tenanted property is that the cost of maintaining a property can be much more accurately determined. Landlord's and agents will find it much more difficult in this instance to play the trick of giving very low 'ball park' figures that in the end turn out to be very wide of the mark. This is because you can you get bills and estimates from both the landlord and the tenants. Make sure that you make the most of this opportunity.

**Could you perhaps find better tenants?** Just 'running' with the tenants that you have inherited can sometimes be a very bad idea. This is because they have become used to a certain way of doing things and also to paying at a certain price level. Significantly changing terms and conditions or raising the rents by more than annual inflation-related increases are therefore likely to elicit very strong protests. You should never assume that, if a property is offered with tenants in situ, it is necessarily the best possible thing to leave them in place. It could very well be that the landlord failed to maximise his returns on investment by hanging on too long to particular tenants.

# Not asking the right legal questions

We have already looked at the importance of having a good solicitor on your team. This can obviously not be emphasised enough. You should remember that a solicitor is often only as effective as the instructions they are given. The ultimate responsibility to ensure that there are no legal problems with a property still rests with you. The solicitor is simply an agent (highly paid at that!) who you appoint to assist you in your investigations and to act on your behalf.

You should, in light of the above, make very sure that your solicitors get answers to the following very important questions:

**Leasehold or Freehold?** This is almost too obvious even to mention, but believe it or not, there are still cases where buyers neglect to state their preference and where often solicitors simply assume that they are aware of the status of the property! This almost borders on criminal neglect as there are huge differences in value and possible usage between the two property classes.

**Rights of Way:** Are there any rights of way attached to the property? If there is a garden at a block of flats, who is allowed to use it? The answers to these kinds of questions can have a huge impact on the value of a property and/or its usefulness as a rental property. You should therefore make very sure that they get asked!

**Alterations to the Property:** Some alterations that may have been undertaken to the property may have required planning permission or buildings regulations consents – for example an attic bedroom or removal of a load-bearing wall, or perhaps a new central heating boiler. Make a note of anything that appears to have been altered and ask your solicitor to investigate whether consents were required, and if necessary for evidence of such consents. Far better to have these checked out before you buy than to have problems with enforcement officers or unstable construction at a later date.

**Usage Restrictions:** There can perhaps be nothing worse than buying a building for a certain purpose and then finding out that it cannot be used in this way. Make sure that your solicitor knows exactly what you want to use a property for and that he/she then researches whether this falls under 'permitted usage' for the particular property.

**Boundaries:** When you buy something you need to know exactly what you are buying. You should therefore be very sure of where a particular property starts and ends and who owns the fences or other boundary markers (e.g. hedges). Having this information at hand is particularly important if you intend to further develop the property at a later stage.

**Marketing Restrictions:** There are sometimes very clear curbs on certain types of marketing techniques. This is especially common in so-called heritage areas. One of the most common restrictions has to do with the putting up of 'For Sale' signs. In some cases this is completely forbidden, while in others the size of the sign is severely restricted. This may not seem like much of a problem but you need to keep in mind that there are certain market conditions where you are going to need all the marketing tactics that you can get!

# Not investigating the possibility of building from scratch

Most people get nightmares at the very mention of a building project but this can actually be an excellent way to achieve a solid return on investment, both as a landlord or if you are 'building to sell'. The main advantages associated with building are the following:

- It is sometimes an easier process than renovating, since you can have significant input at the planning stages. This means that you can get a property that fits your needs from the start.
- It is possible to achieve a very solid return on investment if you sell the property on. Most tenants also have a clear preference for newer properties. Putting a brand new property on the rental market will, therefore, give you something of an edge over the competition.
- Building can, contrary to popular belief, sometimes be very quick. This is especially true in cases where you make use of time saving devices like timber framed kits.

To maximise your profits and rental returns when building you will have to follow a few basic rules. These include:

**Do your utmost to find the best plot:** Land in the UK is in very short supply. This means that good plots at advantageous prices are very scarce. You should, therefore, do a lot of research before taking the final plunge. Try to find a plot in an area with good infrastructure and services. You should also make sure that it is in an area where there is solid demand for new homes.

**Get accurate quotes:** It is very difficult to get quotes for a project that is still in the planning stages. Builders and other tradespersons will sometimes under-quote in order to get the job and then afterwards hike the prices due to 'unforeseen' circumstances or problems. You can avoid this trap by doing a lot of research about average building costs. One way of doing this would be to have a few chats with people who have recently completed projects at the same development.

**Manage and monitor the project:** The main frustrations that people have with the building process often relate to cost and time overruns. Try to avoid this by not merely giving the project over to the builders and contractors and then forgetting about it. Doing so is the closest thing to a recipe for disaster that you are likely to find! Take an active project management approach to the building of your new property. Among other things, this means that you will have to keep a very close eye on schedules, workmanship and budgets.

It obviously takes a certain kind of temperament and skill-set to make a success of a building project. If you think you fit this profile (and have this suspicion confirmed by others!) this could be one of the ways in which you can take your business to the next level!

# Not making use of opportunities for redevelopment

'Regeneration' is one of the buzzwords in the UK property market at the moment. Over the past few years we have seen vast previously derelict areas being reclaimed for residential use. There is no need to assume that the profits to be made from such projects are merely destined for the 'big boys'! Many smaller players, and individual investors, have benefited from the opportunities presented by the redevelopment of inner city and post-industrial areas.

The first step towards becoming involved in redevelopment is, as always, research. Try to find out which areas are 'up and coming'. One of the ways to do this would be to try to find out where the government has already committed significant resources for regeneration and infrastructure development. It goes without saying that you should base your final decision to invest in an area on solid data and not on hearsay and pub talk!

After you have decided on a particular area you should proceed to find a particular property that is within your budget and that you are sure can be redeveloped or modified. After you have done this you should ask yourself the following questions:

- **Can the present structure be used?** It is often possible to use an existing structure in a modified form. The converted warehouses of London's Docklands bear striking testimony to this fact. One of the first things that you should, therefore, do is to get a professional opinion on whether an existing property could be successfully converted and or modified.

- **Are there usage restrictions?** Re-zoning properties for residential use is not generally a problem in designated regeneration areas, since getting people to live there is clearly one of the aims of the whole project. There might be a reason why a particular property is deemed unsuitable for residential purposes. You would obviously be very well advised to make sure whether this is the case or not.

- **What kind of soil are you going to have to deal with?** This is an especially important question if you are thinking of knocking down an existing structure to erect something in its place. Get expert advice to make sure that the kind of soil that you will have to build on will lend itself to residential property development. The main factors to consider are: drainage, ease to build on and suitability for gardening.

- **Are there any environmental issues?** There are certain types of sites and buildings that will first have to be decontaminated before any further development can be undertaken. These include: buildings with asbestos anywhere in the structure (although these are much less common due to concerted efforts to get rid of all known asbestos in the built environment), former filling stations, land near landfill sites and certain kinds of factories. As a smaller investor it would probably be better just to walk away immediately should any contamination be identified, as decontamination can be a very costly and lengthy process.

# Not keeping your eye on national trends

It is so easy to just focus on your own local area and then miss some of the larger social and demographic changes taking place. This should clearly be avoided at all costs, since many changes bring with them fantastic opportunities for the astute. You should, therefore, do your best to study reports, studies and policy changes that could have a direct impact on the housing and commercial property needs in different areas. Some of the things that you should definitely look out for are:

**Areas being designated as 'growth zones':** The population of the UK is projected to increase rapidly over the coming decades, and the government has already started mapping out where it plans to put all the extra people. One way in which this is being done is the designation of certain areas as growth/regeneration zones. Such a designation means that a lot of resources will be put into infrastructure and capacity building. Some of the areas that have been designated include: Ebbsfleet, the Peterborough/Cambridge corridor, Milton Keynes and the 'Thames Gateway'.

**Rapid population growth:** Sometimes the population of a certain town or city increases rapidly over a very short time. The driving forces behind this can be immigration, lifestyle choices and economic opportunities. Entering such a market at exactly the right time can obviously be very advantageous.

**Changes in infrastructure and accessibility:** A new road, bridge or rail line can sometimes change the make-up of an area, as improved access brings with it new people. Try to find out where major infrastructure projects are being undertaken and which communities they are likely to affect.

**Changes in the business and commercial environment:** It is often the case that businesses, government agencies and corporations move offices in search of better facilities, a better trained workforce or cost savings. It is, for example, official policy of the UK Government to move some large government offices into regional cities. The impact of 5000 new workers coming to a regional centre can clearly be significant and you should try your best to be there to ride the wave!

**The impact of tourism:** One of the effects of an area being 'discovered' by tourists is that some of them eventually decide that they want to live in that area. Keeping an eye on the tourist 'hot spots' can, therefore, turn out to be quite an effective strategy in terms of finding new places in which to invest.

# Not being sufficiently prepared when applying for commercial property finance

If you are interested in investing in commercial property you should realise that the process of getting finance to fund your investment can sometimes be much more complicated than is normally the case with residential property. This is because financial institutions rely much less on formulas and templates when making decisions, with the result that much more emphasis will be placed on the individual case. You should, therefore, expect that there will be lots of questions to answer and that thorough checks will be made into your financial and investment track record, as well as into the viability of your business plan.

You can prepare for this by having the following information ready:

- **All relevant personal details:** You will be asked for details of your personal accounts as well as information about personal debts (e.g. mortgages or personal loans). Make sure that you have all such information readily available.

- **Payment records for existing tenants:** Your case will be strengthened if you can show that there are existing tenants in the commercial property who you are considering. It will be even more effective if you can somehow show that the tenants are running viable and profitable businesses from the premises. This can be done through submitting payment records and annual accounts (if tenants are willing to provide them).

- **Property valuation:** You should obviously have the value of the property professionally assessed and you will most probably be asked for a formal commercial surveyors report when you apply for finance.

- **Evidence of your track record as a property investor:** It would be very difficult in the current climate to get finance for commercial property if you were unable to show that you have a successful track record as a property investor. This is because many mortgage companies prefer investors to 'cut their teeth' in the residential market before they move into the commercial arena. You will, therefore, boost your case if you can show that you have been successfully investing in property over a number of years.

Having the above information available will not guarantee that you get the finance that you are asking for. It will, however, help you to get a fair hearing!

# Failing to ensure that your Leasehold Managing Agent has been correctly informed of the Lease transfer

Having completed on the purchase of a leasehold property, it is your solicitor's duty to inform the managing agents of the transfer of the lease and any new charge to be registered. Unfortunately, it is not always a focal point for solicitors. It is one of those tasks which is "left to the end" and is often overlooked, only to come to light some long months later. By this time, service and rent charges will have accrued, and the managing agent will have taken steps to track down the new owner through the Land Registry, and may well have instructed debt collectors. The unfortunate investor may find that he has incurred not only the outstanding management fees accrued during his period of ownership, but also legal fees and administration costs, and his mortgage company may even have become involved too! Obviously this situation is to be avoided at all costs.

Another failure of the solicitor may be that he has registered the transfer of the Lease with the managing agent, but has failed to advise of the investor's correspondence address, again with unfortunate consequences. The managing agent will send all the service charge invoices and reminders to the investment property, where they may well be "binned"! Again, service charges, administration fees and possible legal costs will accrue for the unwitting investor.

Perhaps the best way to avoid these situations is to ask your solicitor to provide you with the name and contact details of the managing agent. Once you have completed on the purchase of your leasehold property, you can then attend to your own damage limitation and inform the managing agents yourself of the transfer – just to get the transaction on record. Make sure that they have your correspondence address and not just the address for the property. Ensure that you confirm any conversation in writing, and keep a copy.

An alternative is to ask your solicitor for a copy of the "Receipt of Notification of Transfer and Charge" which is returned to the solicitor from the managing agent, and is usually a signed duplicate of the solicitor's own notification to the managing agent. It contains such information as your name and correspondence address, together with the property address, details of the transfer (eg parties, completion date, etc), and confirmation of any new chargeholder to be registered. Ensure that all the details are correct.

Finally, look out for expected service charge invoices, and if they do not arrive, contact the managing agent again. Check that the invoices and statements are correct – there may well be a period of apportionment, when the previous owner would have been responsible for service and rent charges up to the day of completion.

# Not maintaining a healthy work-life balance

Many people who enter the world of property investment do so out of a desire to 'kiss their day job goodbye' and to be their own boss. The unfortunate thing is that many of these people end up working much harder than they ever did in salaried employment. It is true that they are now 'their own bosses', but this is perhaps scant consolation when they think back on all the lifestyle benefits that were supposed to have come with being self-employed and which seem to be 'missing in action'. You can avoid this slightly regrettable situation by doing some of the following things:

- **Plan ahead:** If you do not plan your daily and weekly activities your time will just flow towards the 'urgent' at the expense of the important. Avoid this by setting clear priorities for every week and then planning your diary accordingly.
- **Prioritise:** It could be very beneficial to do an 80/20 analysis of your business. The 80/20 principle states that we often spend 80% of our time on activities that generate 20% of our income and vice versa. Write down everything that you do for a week and attach some kind of value to it. You will very soon

see if this is true of you as well. If it is, you need to radically reconfigure your activities.

- **Outsource:** One of the ways in which you can do the 'reconfiguring' above is to hire other people to do some of the things that represent a wasteful use of your time (i.e. doing them is actually causing you to lose money, since they are distracting you from more profitable activities). The rise of the internet has made it possible to outsource a lot of your 'back office' functions to virtual service providers all around the world. This will leave you free to work on maximising your profits and to enjoy the lifestyle that you set out to achieve.

- **Take time out:** It is true that your business requires quality and focused attention. You need to remember, however, that you will not be able to give such attention if you do not step back to enjoy the 'fruits of your labours' every once in the while. Make sure that you take regular short breaks and occasional longer breaks. Doing so will prevent your business from taking over your life in unhealthy ways. Your "downtime" can also serve as very useful time for the incubation of new ideas and strategies. Always ensure that you are running your business and not the other way round.

The tips mentioned above have only scratched the surface of the whole issue of the work-life balance. Make sure that you do some further reading so that it can be said that you are running your business and not the other way around!

# Share in our Success and Enjoy Long-Term Financial Rewards

We've created our own success, now we can help create yours too.

The purpose of Rhett Lewis Property Investments is to improve our customers' incomes by enabling them to share in and benefit from our proven business formulas.

## OUR VALUES

- Open and accessible services
- Continually improving our standards and efficiencies
- Forging a reputation for excellence
- Steady and ongoing business growth
- Unlimited learning opportunities for our employees
- Complete integrity throughout every business transaction

## INVESTMENT

**Portfolio Build – A 'hands free' passive profitable property portfolio**

By building a portfolio, creating a sustainable income through property investment is an achievable dream. Your best approach is to make a good start, with our trusted advice to guide you on your path to property accumulation and ultimately create an income for life.

## CREATING AN INCOME WITH PROPERTY YOU CAN:

- Secure your financial future
- Build a substantial property portfolio
- Generate substantial monthly income in good and bad times

- Minimise your tax bills and accumulate real wealth
- Fund further property opportunities with no deposits

For further information, go to www.rhettlewis.com/ portfoliobuild

### Profit from Private Lending – Generate 15% on your investments

Are you getting frustrated with the small returns you are receiving from bank savings accounts? If the answer is a resounding 'yes', then we can help.

### WHY THIS IS A SOUND INVESTMENT STRATEGY:
- You are in control of the money you invest and how you allocate these funds
- You enjoy fixed returns, with very little risk
- You have control over the length of your investment
- You don't have the inconvenience of administration fees.

For further information, go to www.rhettlewis.com/ profitgenerator

## EDUCATION

### Property Workshop DVD Collection

 A DVD box that contains over 8 hours of essential information that every property investor must know to successfully build and manage a property portfolio.

Each DVD is stacked with powerful strategies for becoming and staying successful, but that is not all, you will also find out and overcome any negative conditioning that has been holding you back from success.

The topics that are covered to :- the mindset and habits of highly successful people, property fundamentals and property planning, 14 ways to find a motivated seller, negotiating 25-40% discounts, how to run your portfolio successfully and more.

For more information, go to www.rhettlewis.com/propertyworkshop

## 'Build your Property Portfolio' Home Study Course

This home study manual is designed to provide working adults and aspiring career professionals with the ability to get additional property education quickly, conveniently and affordably.

There are literally dozens of different ways to make money from property. This probably explains why so many of the great fortunes in history have been built on property and why so many modern day fortunes are based on the same thing.

For more information, go to www.rhettlewis.com/home-study-manual

## 'Become a Property Billionaire' One Day Seminar

This one day seminar offers you the opportunity to incorporate the secrets of billionaire property investors. You will be equipped with a step-by-step PPI system© to achieve financial freedom through property within the next twenty four months.

This seminar will transform your attitude towards property investment, help to boost your income and equip you to maximise profits in all market conditions.

Moreover it will show you how to take advantage of property hotspots, reveal the secrets of how to value a property and explain how to use 'other people's money' to expand your wealth.

Additionally 14 ways to source deals 30-40% below market value are presented and it is demonstrated how to keep buying property and never run out of cash.

For more information, go to <u>www.rhettlewis.com/ billionaire</u>

## Property Mastermind – Mastermind with the experts

A <u>very limited opportunity</u> to become a part of Britain's Leading Property Wealth Group. Only 5 people per quarter are able to become a part of this group.

Becoming a member of this exclusive group provides you with direct access to Rhett Lewis and his World Class inner team of experts and Multi-Millionaire Property Investors.

Moreover, membership offers exclusive access to a fortnightly live and interactive Property Mastermind Telephone Session with Rhett Lewis and leading experts on Property Investing, with exclusive recordings of each fortnight's Telephone Sessions, Weekly Wealth Mastermind Email from Rhett with his personal insights, tips and strategies on Property and Wealth and much more. The value of this membership reaches over £6500.

For more information, go to <u>www.rhettlewis.com/ mastermind</u>

## 1-2-1 Consultation with Rhett

This is your chance to pick the brain of the UK's premier property strategist. For 60 minutes he will give you his undivided attention and you may ask him questions on any topic.

During these 60 minutes on the phone you can expect Rhett's honest and helpful feedback on a leaflet, marketing campaign or anything else that you want him to look at. If you are interested, he can share his 14 ways on how to source below market value properties, Rhett can introduce you to the 12 people you must know to be successful in this game and anything else you may want to talk about that you feel would be helpful to you.

For more information, go to www.rhettlewis.com/1-2-1consult

## 'Become a Property Billionaire' 2 Day Bootcamp

During this 2 day bootcamp the insider secrets, loopholes, tips and strategies to legitimately build a cash flow property portfolio are revealed.

You'll learn everything you ever wanted to know about buying properties without using any of your own money. Other benefits include learning about the 77 big mistakes made by amateur investors, which 6 crucial questions you must ask an estate agent before you agree to view any property, how you can use your contacts to your advantage by getting them to call you first with the juiciest deals and much more.

For more information, go to www.rhettlewis.com/bootcamp

## 'In the Field' Mentorship Day – Your patch or mine

Spend a full day receiving Personal Coaching by Rhett Lewis, a property investment expert.

Rhett will be helping you out, in person and on location, with working out potential deals, setting up your personal power investment team, checking the facts, deciding your strategy, avoiding costly mistakes, making smarter offers, funding your projects and much more.

If you are ready to achieve your goals faster, maximise your profits, close an extremely profitable deal and live your life financially free, then you are ready for your very own mentorship day with Rhett.

For more information, go to www.rhettlewis.com/mentorship